# Understanding and Using MS–DOS/PC–DOS: A Complete Guide

Cody T. Copeland
Jonathan Bacon
Johnson County Community College

**West Publishing Company**
St. Paul          New York          Los Angeles          San Francisco

*Copyeditor:* Chris Thillen
*Cover Design:* Bob Anderson, Computer Arts, Inc.

COPYRIGHT © 1987 by WEST PUBLISHING CO.
    50 W. Kellogg Boulevard
    P.O. Box 64526
    St. Paul, MN 55164-1003

Library of Congress Cataloging-in-Publication Data

Copeland, Cody T.
Understanding and using MS-DOS/PC-DOS.

(The Microcomputing series)
Includes index.
1. MS-DOS (Computer operating systems) 2. PC-DOS
(Computer operating systems) I. Bacon, Jonathan.
II. Title. III. Series.
QA76.76.063C666 1987    005.4;46   86-33963
ISBN 0-314-34747-X

# CONTENTS

**PART I OVERVIEW OF IBM PC-DOS**

**UNIT 1 AN INTRODUCTION TO OPERATING SYSTEMS**

## UNIT 4 FILE MANAGEMENT COMMANDS

## APPLICATION A

# PART III INTERMEDIATE AND ADVANCED DOS COMMANDS

## UNIT 5 THE EDITING DOS COMMAND

## UNIT 6 THE INVISIBLE DOS COMMAND

## UNIT 7 THE HARD DISK MANAGEMENT COMMANDS

## APPLICATION B

## UNIT 8 THE ESOTERIC DOS COMMANDS: REDIRECTION, PIPES, AND FILTERS

## APPLICATION C

## UNIT 9 MORE ESOTERIC DOS COMMANDS: MODE, PRINT, VDISK

## APPLICATION D

## UNIT 10 THE SAFETY DOS COMMANDS

## APPLICATION E

# PUBLISHER'S NOTE

This book is part of THE MICROCOMPUTING SERIES. We are proud to announce that this unique series is now entering its third year, and currently includes four different types of books:

1. A core concepts book, now in its second edition, teaches basic hardware and software applications concepts. This text is titled UNDERSTANDING AND USING MICROCOMPUTERS.

2. A series of introductory level, hands-on workbooks for a wide variety of specific software packages. These provide both self-paced tutorials and complete reference guides. Each book's title begins with UNDERSTANDING AND USING . . . .

3. Several larger volumes combine DOS with three popular software packages. Two of these volumes are called UNDERSTANDING AND USING APPLICATION SOFTWARE, while the third is titled UNDERSTANDING AND USING SHAREWARE APPLICATION SOFTWARE. These versions condense components of the individual workbooks while increasing the coverage of DOS and the integration of different application packages.

4. An advanced level of hands-on workbooks with a strong project/systems orientation. These titles all begin with DEVELOPING AND USING . . . .

Our goal has always been to provide you with maximum flexibility in meeting the changing needs of your courses through this "mix and match" approach. We remain committed to offering the widest variety of current software packages.

We now offer these books in THE MICROCOMPUTING SERIES:

Understanding and Using Microcomputers, second edition     by Steven M. Zimmerman and Leo M. Conrad

## OPERATING SYSTEMS

Understanding and Using MS-DOS/PC DOS:
The First Steps
    by Laura B. Ruff and Mary K. Weitzer

Understanding and Using MS-DOS/PC DOS:
A Complete Guide
    by Cody T. Copeland and Jonathan P. Bacon

## PROGRAMMING LANGUAGES

Understanding and Using Microsoft BASIC/IBM-PC BASIC
    by Mary L. Howard

## WORD PROCESSORS

Understanding and Using Displaywrite 3 and Displaywrite 4
   by Patsy H. Lund and Barbara A. Hayden

Understanding and Using Microsoft Word
   by Jonathan P. Bacon

Understanding and Using MultiMate
   by Mary K. Weitzer and Laura B. Ruff

Understanding and Using PC-Write
   by Victor P. Maiorana

Understanding and Using pfs:WRITE
   by Mary K. Weitzer and Laura B. Ruff

Understanding and Using WordPerfect
   by Patsy H. Lund, Barbara A. Hayden,
   and Sharon S. Larsen

Understanding and Using WordStar
   by Steven C. Ross

Understanding and Using WordStar 4.0
   by Patsy H. Lund and Barbara A. Hayden

## SPREADSHEET PACKAGES

Understanding and Using ExpressCalc (Including PC-CALC)
   by Victor P. Maiorana and Arthur A. Strunk

Understanding and Using Lotus 1-2-3
   by Steven C. Ross

Understanding and Using Lotus 1-2-3 Release 2
   by Steven C. Ross

Understanding and Using SuperCalc 3
   by Steven C. Ross and Judy A. Reinders

Understanding and Using SuperCalc 4
   by Judy A. Reinders and Steven C. Ross

## DATABASE PACKAGES

Understanding and Using dBASE III (Including dBASE II)
   by Steven C. Ross

Understanding and Using dBASE III PLUS
   by Steven C. Ross

Understanding and Using PC-FILE III
   by Victor P. Maiorana and Arthur C. Strunk

Understanding and Using pfs: FILE/REPORT
   by Laura B. Ruff and Mary K. Weitzer

Understanding and Using R:BASE 5000
(Including R:BASE System V)
   by Karen L. Watterson

## INTEGRATED SOFTWARE

Understanding and Using Appleworks (Including AppleWorks 2.0)
   by Frank Short

Understanding and Using Educate-Ability
   by Victor P. Maiorana and Arthur A. Strunk

Understanding and Using FRAMEWORK
   by Karen L. Watterson

Developing and Using Office Applications with AppleWorks
   by M. S. Varnon

Understanding and Using Symphony
   by Enzo V. Allegretti

## COMBINATION VOLUMES

Understanding and Using Application Software, Volume 1:
DOS, WordStar 4.0, Lotus 1-2-3 Release 2, and dBASE III Plus
   by Patsy H. Lund, Barbara A. Hayden, and Steven C. Ross

Understanding and Using Application Software, Volume 2:
DOS, WordPerfect, Lotus 1-2-3 Release 2, and dBASE III Plus
   by Patsy H. Lund, Barbara A. Hayden, and Steven C. Ross

Understanding and Using SHAREWARE Application Software:
DOS, PC-Write, ExpressCalc, and PC-FILE
   by Victor P. Maiorana and Arthur A. Strunk

## ADVANCED BOOKS

Developing and Using Advanced Lotus 1-2-3 Applications
   by Steven C. Ross

Developing and Using Decision Support Applications
   by Steven C. Ross, Richard J. Penlesky, and Lloyd D. Doney

Developing and Using Micrcomputer Business Systems
   by Kathryn W. Huff

We are delighted by the popularity of THE MICROCOMPUTING SERIES. We appreciate your support, and look forward to your suggestions and comments. Please write to us at this address:

*West Publishing Company*
*College Division*
50 West Kellogg Blvd. P.O. Box 64526 St. Paul, MN 55164

# ABOUT THE AUTHORS

**ABOUT THE AUTHORS**

Jonathan Bacon holds a Bachelor of Arts degree in English Literature and a Master of Arts degree in Student Personnel Work, both from Michigan State University at East Lansing. He has also completed more than 30 hours in data processing. His experience includes designing the Introduction to Personal Computers credit course at Johnson County Community College. He has also authored or co-authored over ten step-by-step manuals for the college's Microcomputer Training Center, covering such topics as Lotus 1-2-3, PC-DOS, Multimate, MultiPlan, PFS:FILE, PFS:Write, Smart System software, and WordStar.

Bacon is currently the Manager of Administrative Student Data Processing Systems at Johnson County Community College. He formerly served as the Director of Student Development and Counseling at the college.

Cody T. Copeland holds a Bachelor of Education degree from the University of Arizona at Tucson and a Master of Education degree from the University of Wyoming at Laramie. He has been involved in technical training for the last ten years, in the fields of aviation and microcomputers.

Copeland developed and initiated the Johnson County Community College Microcomputer Training Center shortly after arriving there in 1982. The center currently trains over two thousand business and industry students each year. He has written training materials for courses on Symphony, Introduction to Personal Computers, the Smart System, and Lotus 1-2-3.

Both Bacon and Copeland were instrumental in developing the curriculum for the Johnson County Community College Microcomputer Training Center, and have done extensive training for students, staff, and community members as well as corporate employees.

# PREFACE

## WHO SHOULD USE THIS BOOK?

Welcome to *Understanding and Using MS-DOS/PC-DOS: A Complete Guide*. This book is designed to meet the needs of both students and instructors, both novice and experienced users--those have managed to avoid learning DOS. Whether you are a student, instructor, corporate manager, secretary, or a home user, this book is intended to familiarize you with the mysteries of the IBM PC operating system.

Our aim is to introduce you to new concepts regarding DOS, one at a time. After some explanatory text, we'll follow up with step-by-step guided activities to make the new concepts and skills clear. We believe in hands-on learning--with computers there is no other way.

## CONTENT HIGHLIGHTS

*Understanding and Using MS-DOS/PC-DOS* is divided into three parts. Part I introduces you to operating systems and explains what they are. Part II then explores the fundamental DOS commands; it is followed in Part III with an exploration of intermediate and advanced DOS commands. You may be tempted to overlook Part I because it is straight reading. Please resist that temptation unless you have had previous exposure to the basics of DOS. Keep in mind that the terms defined and the concepts explained in that part of the book are essential to understanding the subsequent guided activities.

With the exception of Part I, this book is meant to be read while seated in front of your computer, so you can complete the step-by-step guided activities.  Each unit includes several important segments.

Supplies Needed
Objectives
Important Commands
Assignments
Review Questions
Documentation Research

Additionally, most units include one or more guided activities preceded by explanatory text.  To complete all guided activities in the text, the student or reader will need a DOS diskette, preferably PC-DOS 3.x; six (6) blank double sided double density diskettes and access to the IBM DISK OPERATING SYSTEM version 3.1 manual or other MS-DOS or PC-DOS manual.  Equipment needed is covered in a later section of this Preface.

If using this text in a classroom setting, your instructor will indicate which assignments, review questions and documentation research will be assigned for the units covered.

All documentation research questions are based upon use of the IBM DISK OPERATING SYSTEM version 3.1 manual.  Other versions of the manual may be used, but the chapter references will not apply. When using another version, scan the table of contents for topics similar to those suggested in the documentation research.

## APPROACH TO THE TEXT

This text has been constructed to allow the instructor and student to select the units and assignments most appropriate for their needs.  Each unit includes numerous assignments, review questions and documentation research.  The text is written to build from scratch with each subsequent unit building on concepts presented in previous units.  However, a pick and chose approach may be just as appropriate for students with previous computing experience.

A beginning course on DOS might only concentrate on units 1, 2, 3, 4, 5, 6, 7 and 13.  Advanced users might wish to jump right into units 7, 8, 9, 10, and 13.  Unit 11 is a strange creature.  Without a network and a network operating system, it is difficult to complete any hands-on exercise.  Instead the authors have decided to simply introduce some network concepts.

Unit 12 is more than a discussion of DOS shells, it is a synthesis of commands covered throughout the text.  The long exercise in this chapter builds a simple DOS shell composed of numerous batch files.  The process of building the shell acts as a review of numerous commands including Backup, Cls, Copy, Echo, Edlin, Format, Mkdir, Pause, Prompt and Type.  The shell constructed is very simple when compared with commercially available software.  However, the exercise is realistic in that numerous DOS commands are strung together to accomplish typical file management tasks.

Although Edlin is covered in unit 5, some students may prefer to use a word processor which generates an ASCII text file.  We have covered Edlin in depth for two reasons:  First, it comes free with IBM PC-DOS and second, it is often the easiest method of editing a small text file quickly.  The guided activities in unit 6 and subsequent units are designed to use Edlin.  The same files may be created using a word processor but the authors strongly urge the use of Edlin.  Even though it is a quick and dirty line editor with few bells and whistles...it still is a standard to which students should be exposed.

## COMPUTER TERMS DICTIONARY

Appendix A is a comprehensive dictionary of computer terms.  Without turning the entire text into a dictionary, it is not always possible to define terms as they are introduced--though we have tried to do so. We have used boldface to alert the reader to check the Computer Terms Dictionary.  Where appropriate, each unit lists dictionary terms to be reviewed under assignments.

## VERSIONS OF DOS

Screens and examples used through out this text are based on PC-DOS version 3.x.  Software designers, developers and users typically use the **x** to designate any version in the series.  For instance, 3.x refers to any one of several versions of DOS which compose the third major revision (i.e., 3.0, 3.1. 3.2 or 3.21). DOS 3.x is the most recent major version available at this writing.  However, most of the guided activities within the units may be accomplished using older versions of PC-DOS or MS-DOS.  Where differences exist, we have attempted to point them out.

## HARDWARE NEEDED

Guided activities in this text have been written for the IBM PC, XT, AT or 100% compatible.  We understand that many readers may be using personal computers created by manufacturers other than IBM.  These machines are typically referred to as compatibles or clones.  The guided activities can be completed successfully on any 100% IBM compatible machine.  Where differences exist, we have tried to note them within the text.

Except where noted, all guided activities within the text may be completed using a two floppy disk drive system with at least 512 Kilobytes of RAM, a printer, and either a monochrome or color monitor.  One major exception is the guided activity in unit 12.  The creation of the sample DOS shell requires access to an IBM PC/XT or compatible with at least one floppy disk drive and a hard disk.

## ACKNOWLEDGEMENTS

Our thanks must first go to editor Richard Wohl, who prompted, prodded and encouraged the authors through out the creative process. Thanks also to production assistant Cheryl Wilms. She provided a great deal of telephone consultation to keep the authors on track.

We were very fortunate to have the participation of five excellent reviewers. The expertise, time and effort of these reviewers was essential in shaping the final draft of this book. We wish to express our gratitude to:

Terry S. Dorsett
Central Arizona College

Jack T. Hogue
The University of North Carolina at Charlotte

John Morack
Waukesha County Technical Institute

George Upchurch
Carson-Newman College

Jack van Luik
Mt. Hood Community College

Throughout the preparation of this manuscript, the authors have appreciated the opportunity provided by the administration of Johnson County Community College who clearly support excellence, individual creativity and publication by staff members. In addition to the Board of Trustees, the authors would like to specifically acknowledge the following administrators: Dr. Charles J. Carlsen, President; Dr. Dan Radakovich, Vice President for Academic Affairs; Dr. Gerald Baird, Vice President Administrative Services; Dr. Linda L. Dayton, Dean of Student Services; and Mr. Dane Lonborg, Dean of Community Education.

The authors appreciate the telephone consultation provided by Wanda Volpe and David Guest of Beaman Porter, Inc. of Harrison, New York. Their assistance with the PowerText Formatter: Automatic DeskTop Publishing Software was invaluable.

Cody Copeland would like to thank Susan, Tyler, Matthew and Jeremy Copeland; "who have allowed a hobby to consume me. Also special thanks to my Mother, Lucille F. Copeland."

Jonathan Bacon would like to thank "the three young women who provide inspiration in my life; Joan, Jennifer and Jodi Bacon. Also a special thanks to my Father, Paul J. Bacon for his continual support."

# 1

# OVERVIEW OF IBM PC-DOS

This is the first of three parts in this text. In this part, we offer a general overview of IBM PC-DOS and its sister operating system, MS-DOS. We discuss the basic function of a microcomputer operating system, provide a brief history of PC-DOS and MS-DOS, computer language syntax and discuss internal versus external DOS commands. This first part concludes with a discussion of basic concepts of DOS including filenames, extensions, wildcard characters, and drive designations.

Once this background information is covered, we can proceed to discuss the most commonly used DOS commands. Toward the end of unit 1, we provide a short listing of the most commonly used DOS commands, their uses, and syntax. Additional commands will be covered in subsequent units, but for the novice these common commands are of primary importance.

Subsequently in Part II, we lead you through guided activities using these commands. In Part III, we cover additional topics which are only mentioned in this initial overview. Topics to be covered later in greater detail include multitasking, multiprocessing, archiving (backing up) files, expanded verses extended memory, and networks.

UNIT

# 1

# AN INTRODUCTION TO OPERATING SYSTEMS

**SUPPLIES NEEDED**

The supplies that you will need for completing this unit are:

1. IBM DISK OPERATING SYSTEM version 3.1 manual.

Note: This unit does not require access to a microcomputer.

**OBJECTIVES**

After completing this unit, you will be able to:

1. explain the function of a microcomputer disk operating system;
2. explain the process followed when a computer is booted;
3. list the differences between MS-DOS and PC-DOS;
4. understand the concept of computer language syntax;
5. understand the difference between internal and external DOS commands;
6. list the guidelines for creating filenames under DOS;
7. define the different parts of a filename;
8. recognize legal DOS filenames.

## ASSIGNMENTS

Place a check in front of the assignments assigned to you by your instructor. The assignments to be completed for this unit are:

1.____ Review and understand the following computer terms listed in the Computer Terms Dictionary (Appendix A): archive, basic input/output system, boot, compatibles, complete filename, CPU, DOS prompt, external DOS commands, drive designation, extension, file specification, filename, input, internal DOS commands, output, parameters, peripherals, POST, RAM, ROM, switch, and wildcard characters.
2.____ Review Questions.
3.____ Documentation Research.


## AN INTRODUCTION TO OPERATING SYSTEMS

Computer users are usually familiar with the types of business software on the market; that is, word processors, spreadsheet software, and data base management software. Additional application programs exist to facilitate telecommunications, time management, accounting, payroll management, inventory, decision-making support, and a host of other functions. Software manufacturers vie for the attention of users.

One category of software sits in the background on a shelf. No one gets excited about this most fundamental software, yet without it, application software is useless. Without this forgotten software the **central processing unit** (CPU), the heart of the computer system, cannot communicate with attached peripherals (printers, modems, etc.) and input cannot be accepted from the keyboard nor output displayed on the monitor screen.

New microcomputer owners have been known to cart home a system unit, monitor, printer, cables, and tons of software, yet neglect to purchase this oft-forgotten software.

On the surface, microcomputers appear to be miraculous little machines with secretive insides. Even for the moderately computer-literate person it may seem as if putting a floppy disk in the drive and hitting the appropriate keystroke is the totality of this new science. There is neither magic nor mystery in the system unit. Microcomputers need instructions in order to function. Someone or something must provide meticulous, step-by-step instructions to tell the micro how to behave like a computer.

In the world of mainframe computers, these instructions are referred to as the **operating system** (OS). The OS must kick into operation from the second the computer system is powered up and handle additional instructions as required. The computer must know how to respond to keyboard input, read directions from memory or a storage device (like a diskette), and wait for further instructions. From a mainframe point of view, a subset of the operating system is the **disk operating system** (DOS). DOS handles only the basic input and output operations between the CPU and the disk drives.

In the world of microcomputers, the operating system has become synonymous with DOS, which rhymes with "boss." When referring to DOS, most microcomputer users are talking about the entire operating system.

The IBM **Personal Computer** (PC) family of microcomputers and **compatibles** use what is referred to as IBM **Personal Computer DOS** (PC-DOS) or **Microsoft DOS** (MS-DOS). Microsoft is the firm which developed PC-DOS for IBM computers and MS-DOS for manufacturers of compatibles.

Word processors, data managers, accounting programs, and all other software is written to run with a specific operating system. Operating systems in turn are written to take advantage of a specific microprocessor. The following machines use the microprocessors listed:

Apple computers          MOS Technology 6502 and 65C02
Commodore Amiga          Motorola 68000
IBM PC, XT, AT           Intel 8088, 80286 and 80386

Software written for the Apple or other non-IBM compatible machine will not run on the IBM PC unless it is rewritten to use the IBM OS and hardware. The reverse is also true.

Compatibles exist because their manufacturers use the same basic operating system, or one which closely duplicates the operating system's set of instructions. Part of DOS, called the **Basic Input/Output System** (BIOS) is contained in **read only memory** (ROM). ROM microchips contain tiny etched circuitry with embedded instructions. Each time electric current surges through the circuitry, the same instructions are generated. Some of these ROM chips include the instructions which form BIOS, or the interface between the OS and the specific hardware being used. This portion of the OS is so automatic that most users rarely concern themselves with it.

## THE POWER-ON SELF-TEST

An example of a ROM-based portion of DOS is the **power-on self-test** (POST). When an IBM PC is initially booted, it conducts a power-on self-test which takes 3 to 90 seconds (depending upon how much random access memory (RAM) is installed in the computer). It checks memory and tries to assure that the system is okay before proceeding. With an IBM microcomputer if everything is functional, the system generates a single beep. A second beep means a problem was encountered, such as a bad memory chip, unattached keyboard or some other problem. IBM compatibles respond differently. They may not beep, but rather display an error message on the monitor screen.

The instructions for POST are included in ROM. Time after time, year after year, the computer will follow these instructions every time the system is booted. The POST is part of the operating system.

After POST is completed, DOS instructs the computer to check disk drive A: for instructions. You will note that the red in-use light on drive A: lights up at this point. If instructions are found on a disk, the computer reads them. If no disk is in the drive (and the system includes a hard-disk), then DOS checks drive C: (the hard-disk) for instructions. On an IBM computer, if computer-readable instructions are still not found, DOS takes over again and reads a version of IBM Personal Computer **Beginner's All-Purpose Symbolic Instruction Code** (BASIC) into memory. This version of BASIC is also stored in ROM. On IBM compatibles or clones, other responses may be encountered. The most common is an error message indicating that no disk in in the disk drive. Typically manufacturers of PC clones do not include IBM or Microsoft BASIC because it is a proprietary software. The licensing fees for including the software in ROM, even if available, would increase the cost of the machine.

In one exercise, you will see POST at work. This manual, however, will not cover the IBM PC BASIC language. It is used for programming the computer to complete specific tasks.

When the computer goes to drive A: and then subsequently to drive C:, it is looking for additional instructions or additional specialized portions of the software called DOS. The specific files DOS is looking for will be covered later in this unit.

## THE IMPORTANCE OF THE DISK OPERATING SYSTEM

DOS is the most crucial software any user will ever own. Without it, the IBM Personal Computer can only sit and look pretty. DOS has variously been described as a go-between, a traffic cop, or the manager of the computer. In fact, DOS is the manager of communications (or data transfer) between the computer and its internal/external parts such as memory, printers, disk drives, and video display. Figure 1-1 shows some of the functions performed by the operating system.

The operating system handles basic instructions such as telling the computer how to retrieve, store, or delete data from the disk. Although these instructions are written in machine language, the same operation can be accessed by a software package or by the user via the computer keyboard input of DOS commands such as Copy, Pause, and Erase.

Even if a user intends to only use prepackaged software, a basic understanding of DOS commands is essential. Without understanding DOS, you cannot do even simple maintenance activities such as making duplicates of data or application program diskettes.

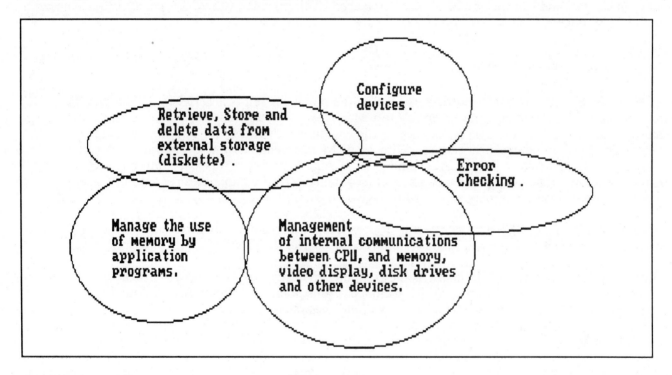

FIGURE 1-1. Functions of the Operating System.

## A CONCISE HISTORY OF DOS

PC-DOS was developed by Microsoft Corporation as an operating system for IBM. The original version (DOS 1.0) supported floppy drive systems only. When the IBM Personal Computer was introduced in the spring of 1981, only floppy-based systems were available. The operating system developed by Microsoft for IBM is technically referred to as IBM DOS. PC-DOS doesn't exist, except as a nickname assigned by users. As soon as PC-DOS 1.0 became available, a similar product was simultaneously offered by Microsoft. It was licensed to other vendors and the general public as MS-DOS.

By the time hard-disk drives were available for the PC XT, DOS 2.0 was available. It provided additional commands which supported the use of hard drive systems. In early 1986, DOS 3.0 became available to add yet another dimension to the IBM family of computers. DOS 3.0 was the first version to support the networking of several microcomputers. Networking is simply the process of linking several microcomputers together so that files and data may be shared. Networks will be covered in a later unit. A comparison of features and fixes provided by each version of DOS is provided in Figure 1-2.

Late in March 1986, IBM announced the release of DOS 3.20. This controversial version of the operating system found many users taking a wait-and-see approach. Though it contained several new features, including Xcopy.exe, Replace.exe, Exdskbio.com, Driver.sys, and an enhanced Format.exe command, PC users generally chose to wait for the unannounced DOS 5.0 due in early 1987. DOS 3.20 did provide additional support for the IBM Token-Ring Network. Additional detail on DOS 3.2 and higher is provided in the final chapter on The Future of IBM PC-DOS.

The "breakthrough" DOS is expected to be 5.0 because of two new enhancements. First, it will be able to address up to 16 megabytes of memory, compared to 640 **kilobytes** (K) with earlier versions of DOS. Second, DOS 5.0 is expected to be the first true multitasking IBM micro-based operating system. Multitasking is the capability of a micro to manage more than one activity or operation at a time. An example would be the capability to sort extensive records in the background (a part of memory set aside for such a function) while the user continues working with another application in the foreground.

Additional information on multitasking, multiprocessing, networking, background, and foreground tasks is presented in later chapters. Do not be overly concerned with these topics yet.

**Version 1.0**

Did not support serial communication : Had bugs in BASIC : Supported single sided diskettes (8 sectors per track) : Date & Time commands were external : Files were only date (not time) stamped : Supported IBM PC

**Version 1.05**

Fixed BASIC bugs

**Version 1.1**

Mode command supported serial communications : Supported double sided diskettes (8 sectors per track) : Date & Time commands became internal : Files were date & time stamped : Verification and file concatenation added to Copy command : Exe2bin program added for programmers : Officially retired by IBM in 1985

**Version 2.0**

Hard disk management commands added : Supported IBM XT

**Version 2.1**

Corrected bugs in 2.0 : Added support for PC Jr : Added support for half height disk drives

**Version 3.0**

Supports quad-density diskettes : Can configure keyboard to country of use : Can configure time & date display : Supports display of foreign graphic characters and characters with an ASCII value greater than 127 : Supports file-sharing and networking : Supports RAM disk : Supports IBM AT

**Version 3.1**

Commands added to reassign or combine drives and directories : Commands enhanced to work with LANs. Plus specific support for PC Token-Ring Network added

**Version 3.2**

Support added for 3.5 inch (720K) diskette : Enhanced new commands to work with 720K diskette and added safety features to Format command : Adds the Replace command to selectively replace files on a target disk with files of the same name on the source diskette

FIGURE 1-2. Comparison Chart of DOS 1.0 through 3.2

## DIFFERENCES BETWEEN PC-DOS AND MS-DOS

Although the two versions of DOS used by IBM and manufacturers of IBM-compatible computers are basically the same, there are some differences.  Rather than deal with historic differences, let's examine those differences as evidenced in DOS version 3.0.

MS-DOS is the generic product, whereas PC-DOS has been customized to create a machine-specific product for the IBM line, which includes the IBM PC, IBM XT, and IBM AT.  MS-DOS is the Chevy version while PC-DOS is the Cadillac.  Both products will get you from "here" to "there," but PC-DOS has some additional bells and whistles.

The additional features will be covered in greater detail later, but here we only list the additional capabilities.  PC-DOS 3.0 provided the following features, which were not available with MS-DOS version 3.0.

1. Compare two disks (Diskcomp);
2. Display directories and subdirectories (Tree);
3. Reassign disk drives (Assign);
4. Dump a graphics screen to the printer (Graphics);
5. Switch modes from color to mono, serial to parallel (Mode);
6. Share files between multiple PCs on a network (Share).

Beginning with MS-DOS version 2.11, MicroSoft has attempted to standardize both versions of DOS. PC-DOS 2.1 and MS-DOS 2.11 are essentially the same.  If a new version of PC-DOS adds features, then the subsequent version of MS-DOS plays catch-up.  Most observers anticipate that any differences between MS-DOS and PC-DOS are only temporary, unless IBM decides to become more restrictive with its operating system.

## COMPUTER LANGUAGE SYNTAX: THE ORDER WHICH PROMOTES UNDERSTANDING

English, French, German, and any other spoken or written language requires that users follow certain conventions.  There are rules for singular versus plural subjects.  Guidelines define what is present tense or past tense.  Even the syntax or order of the language is important.

Syntax is simply the way in which words, phrases, and ideas are put together, either verbally or on paper. We must use language to communicate with computers; and because the machine is limited in understanding, the syntax with computers is even more exacting.  We cannot assume the machine can guess our intentions based upon body language, voice inflections, or familiarity.

An example of using syntax in the English language might clarify its use with computers.  Wayne, Susan and Phil, are watching television when Susan becomes overwhelmed with a thirst for cola.  She knows the refrigerator is bereft of cola.  Susan says "get," but the obvious question is "get what?".  To clarify the command, the Susan says, "get a cola."  Further clarification is still needed.  Is she offering Phil and Wayne a cola, and if so, where are the colas?

The command must be expanded to include "get me a cola," and yet she still has not clarified where the cola is.  Further, who is Susan talking to?  Will Phil or Wayne get the cola?  In computerese, those additional modifiers are called **parameters**.  Susan's problem is the lack of modifiers or parameters. Another problem might be the sequence in which she states the command.

The following commands include the same words, and though one sounds like baby talk, the meanings are clear but very different:

"Wayne go to the store and get me a cola."
"Me go to the store and get Wayne a cola."

Further, if the same words would probably be indecipherable if ordered as:

"Store to Wayne the go me cola a get and."

Syntax makes all the difference.  The same words are used, but in this phrase their order defies meaning.

Computer language syntax must follow a specified order or the computer is left saying "Bad Command or Filename"...its equivalent of "huh??".  Commands must be modified by the use of parameters.

In the following command form (which is also referred to as a command line), everything after the command "Copy" is a parameter or **switch**.

COPY a:FILE_A b:FILE_A

It says to the computer, copy the file named "FILE_A" from the disk in drive A: to the disk in drive B:.  It might be helpful to note that with DOS, if two filenames are listed on a command line, the first is always a source file and the second is the target.  This is a PC-DOS/MS-DOS syntax standard.  It may be helpful to consider the first file as the FROM file and the second one as the TO file.  So in the above example, the copy is FROM a:FILE_A TO b:FILE_A.  If a file were being renamed the Ren command may be used.  To change the file from HELP to ASSIST would require the following command line:

REN a:HELP a:ASSIST

NOTE FOR FORMER CP/M USERS:  For readers who may be familiar with the CP/M operating system, the syntax in PC-DOS and MS-DOS is the reverse of what you might expect.  CP/M used the syntax standard of COPY TO FROM rather than DOS's convention of COPY FROM TO.  Just be aware of the difference.

When communicating with DOS, certain rules of the language must be followed.  As we discuss DOS commands and use syntax diagrams, please note that items listed in brackets [ ] are optional.  Even though optional, they may be required to accomplish the task at hand.  For instance, a file cannot be copied from drive A: to drive B: without using the optional drive name parameters.  The drive name is optional because we could copy a file on a disk in drive a: under one name to the same disk under another filename.  This example will be clarified further when we deal with the Copy command.

Though DOS commands and parameters may be listed in uppercase, DOS is not case-sensitive. DOS commands and parameters may be entered in either upper- or lowercase from the keyboard.

In each syntax diagram, the following abbreviations will be used.

d: represents a disk drive name, such as the a: or b: drive. DOS parameters are not case-sensitive; they may be upper- or lowercase so A: or B: is also acceptable. If the computer system has a hard-disk, it is usually referred to as drive c: (or C:).

s: represents the source disk; for example, in the Copy command, the disk from which a copy is being made.

t: represents the target diskette; for example, in the Copy command, the disk to which a copy is being made.

In most DOS operations, the original diskette is called the **source** and the recipient of a specific DOS operation is the **target** diskette.

## ALPHABETICAL LIST OF COMMON DOS COMMANDS

The following syntax diagrams and brief definitions cover the most commonly used DOS commands. Each command will be discussed in more detail in subsequent chapters.

| | |
|---|---|
| Chdir [directory] | Changes or switches from one subdirectory to another on a disk or hard-disk. The short form or mnemonic form of this command is Cd. |
| Chkdsk [d:] | Checks the disk in the default drive (or in the drive specified by the parameter) for available memory. Also indicates total disk space available in bytes and bytes used. |
| Cls | Clears the monitor screen of everything except for DOS prompt (i.e., A:> ). |
| Comp [d:]filename [d:]filename | Compares the contents of two files to determine if they are identical. Used commonly after Copy command. |
| Copy [s:]filename [t:]filename | Copies file(s) indicated. Can duplicate from one disk to another or copy the contents of one file to another (with a new filename) on the same disk. |
| Date | Displays the current date, if entered when the system was first booted. This command can be used to change the date held in memory by the computer. |
| Del [d:]filename | Erases the specified file from the disk in the default drive (or drive specified by the parameter). |

| | |
|---|---|
| Dir [d:] | Lists files on the default drive or on the drive specified by the parameter used. |
| Diskcomp [d:] [d:] | Compares files on two disks to determine if they are identical. Commonly used after Diskcopy to assure that all files copied correctly. |
| Diskcopy [s:] [t:] | Copies all files from one disk to another. Automatically formats the target disk before copying. |
| Erase [d:]filename | See Del. |
| Format [d:] | Initializes the disk in the default drive or drive specified by a parameter. The Format command prepares the surface of the disk for use by the computer. Without formatting, the disk cannot store files. All disks must be formatted with either the Diskcopy or Format command before use. An important point: this command erases anything on a disk or hard-disk. Once erased, the material is not retrievable. USE CAUTION! |
| Mkdir [directory] | Makes or creates a new directory or subdirectory. The short or mnemonic form of this command is Md. |
| Path | Gives the user access to files in a subdirectory other than the current one. |
| Ren [d:]oldfilename [d:]newfilename | Renames a file. Both the old and new filenames must be specified. Drives need to be specified only if one or both of the files are in a drive other than the default drive. |
| Rmdir [directory] | Removes or destroys a subdirectory. The short or mnemonic form of this command is Rd. |
| Rename [d:]oldname [d:]newname | See Ren. |
| Time | Displays the current time, if entered when the system was booted. This command also allows the user to change the time retained by the system. |
| Type [d:]filename | Displays contents of a specified file on the standard output device (typically the monitor screen). This command works only with standard ASCII files. Control characters used by software packages will be displayed as graphic characters. |
| Ver | Displays the version number (i.e., 2.0, 2.1, 3.1, or 3.2) of DOS loaded into the computer's memory. |

## INTERNAL VERSUS EXTERNAL DOS COMMANDS

Perhaps the most difficult concept for the new microcomputer user is the concept of internal versus external DOS commands.  When we discuss filename extensions later in this unit, it will be disclosed that files with a .Com or .Exe extension on the DOS disk are external commands.  In this usage, external simply means that the command must be read from disk in order to be executed.  It is external to working memory (RAM) until the file is read into memory.

Internal DOS commands, on the other hand, are always resident in working memory.  By working memory, we mean **random access memory** (RAM).  The original IBM PC came with 64K.  The more recent Revision "B" PC includes a minimum of 256 kilobytes of memory, and can be upgraded to 640K. 640K is the maximum memory addressable at one time by the 8086 or 8088 microprocessor and DOS versions 3.x and earlier.  A portion of that memory is consumed by loading DOS.  The COMMAND.COM file includes instructions for the DOS command processor (i.e., that "thing" which processes commands).  With PC-DOS, COMMAND.COM automatically loads IBMBIO.COM and IBMDOS.COM, two hidden files which contain additional portions of DOS.  Once they are loaded, the internal DOS commands are accessible from the keyboard.

---

An important note: both internal and external DOS commands are available only when the DOS prompt ( A> or B> or C>) is displayed on the screen.  That prompt literally means: "ready for your command."

---

## LIST OF INTERNAL DOS COMMANDS

Here is a list of all internal DOS commands. Each will be discussed later. Do not be concerned with what each command does yet. Save that for future units. Use this list only as a reference guide. Remember that these commands may be used whenever the DOS prompt appears. They are automatically loaded into memory at the initial boot.

DOS commands are printed in upper and lowercase throughout this text. This is to emphasize that DOS commands are not case-sensitive. They may be entered in upper- or lowercase, or a combination of the two.

In going from DOS 1.0 to 3.0, some changes in internal commands have been made. As a historical record, note the expansion of available DOS commands with each new version.

| DOS 1.1 | DOS 2.0 | DOS 3.1 | DOS 3.2 |
|---------|---------|---------|---------|
| (Batch) | (Batch) | (Batch) | (Batch) |
|  | Break | Break | Break |
|  | Chdir or Cd | Chdir or Cd | Chdir or Cd |
|  | Cls | Cls | Cls |
| Copy | Copy | Copy | Copy |
|  |  | Ctty | Ctty |
| Date | Date* | Date* | Date* |
|  | Del | Del | Del |
| Dir | Dir | Dir | Dir |
|  | Echo | Echo | Echo |
| Erase | Erase | Erase | Erase |
|  | For | For | For |
|  | Goto | Goto | Goto |
|  | If | If | If |
|  | Mkdir or Md | Mkdir or Md | Mkdir or Md |
|  | Path | Path | Path |
| Pause | Pause | Pause | Pause |
|  |  | Prompt | Prompt |
| Rem | Rem | Rem | Rem |
|  | Ren | Ren | Ren |
| Rename | Rename | Rename | Rename |
|  | Rmdir or Rd | Rmdir or Rd | Rmdir or Rd |
|  | Set | Set | Set |
|  | Shift | Shift | Shift |
| Time | Time | Time | Time |
| Type | Type | Type | Type |
|  | Ver | Ver | Ver |
|  | Verify | Verify | Verify |
|  | Vol | Vol | Vol |

* Note: In DOS 1.0 these were external commands.

## LIST OF EXTERNAL DOS COMMANDS

The following are external DOS commands* which will be discussed within this text. Use this table as a reference guide. External DOS commands may be executed whenever the DOS prompt appears only if the corresponding DOS file is in the default drive, that is, Diskcomp cannot be used unless the DISKCOMP.COM file can be accessed by the computer. These files are not automatically loaded into memory when the system boots.

| DOS 1.1 | DOS 2.0 | DOS 3.1 | DOS 3.2 |
|---------|---------|---------|---------|
|         | Assign  | Assign  | Assign  |
|         |         | Attrib  | Attrib  |
|         | Backup  | Backup  | Backup  |
| Chkdsk  | Chkdsk  | Chkdsk  | Chkdsk  |
| Comp    | Comp    | Comp    | Comp    |
|         | Debug   | Debug   | Debug   |
| Diskcomp | Diskcomp | Diskcomp | Diskcomp |
| Diskcopy | Diskcopy | Diskcopy | Diskcopy |
|         |         |         | Driver  |
| Exe2bin | Exe2bin | Exe2bin | Exe2bin |
|         | Edlin   | Edlin   | Edlin   |
|         | Fdisk   | Fdisk   | Fdisk   |
|         |         | Find    | Find    |
| Format  | Format  | Format  | Format  |
|         |         | Graftabl | Graftabl |
|         | Graphics | Graphics | Graphics |
|         |         | Join    | Join    |
|         |         | Keybfr  | Keybfr  |
|         |         | Keybgr  | Keybgr  |
|         |         | Keybit  | Keybit  |
|         |         | Keybsp  | Keybsp  |
|         |         | Keybuk  | Keybuk  |
|         |         | Label   | Label   |
| Mode    | Mode    | Mode    | Mode    |
|         |         | More    | More    |
|         | Print   | Print   | Print   |
|         | Recover | Recover | Recover |
|         |         |         | Replace |
|         | Restore | Restore | Restore |
|         |         | Select  | Select  |
|         |         | Share   | Share   |
|         |         | Sort    | Sort    |
|         |         | Subst   | Subst   |
| Sys     | Sys     | Sys     | Sys     |
|         | Tree    | Tree    | Tree    |
|         |         | Vdisk   | Vdisk   |
|         |         |         | Xcopy   |

* DOS must first read these files from disk, then it can execute the instructions contained in the file.

## LEGAL FILENAMES, EXTENSIONS AND DRIVE DESIGNATORS

Guidelines for **filenames** must be understood before proceeding to discuss specific DOS commands. Even beginning computer users must use filenames. They are unavoidable. Every time data is saved to disk, or an application program (like a word processor) is loaded, a filename must be used. The filename is composed of three parts:

1. the drive designation,
2. the file specification (often referred to as the filename),
3. the extension.

## THE FILE SPECIFICATION

DOS 2.1 and later versions use the following guidelines for the file specification. Filenames are used with DOS to identify specific data, text, or application files. A file specification must be no longer than eight characters. The following groups of characters may be used in a file specification:

| | |
|---|---|
| capital alphabetic characters | A-Z |
| lowercase alphabetic characters | a-z |
| numeric characters | 0-9 |
| special characters | ! @ # $ % & ( ) - _ { } ' ' |

Following the above guidelines, legal filenames could include:

&G#$DX98
HUH!
PICKLES

File specifications should be descriptive of the contents of the file they identify. Thus, PICKLES would be an acceptable file specification for a letter of complaint regarding a spoiled jar of pickles purchased at a produce store. The first two file specifications are not very descriptive of the file's contents, even though they are legal file specifications.

Special characters are often avoided in the entire filename, unless absolutely necessary. They seldom add much description to a file specification.

**THE FILENAME EXTENSION**

The extension is a one, two or three-character add-on to the file specification. It is not required, but often helpful. The extension always follows a delimiter (i.e., a period) and is tacked onto the end of the file specification. Legal filenames with extensions would include:

LETTER.doc
Cost.ws
Order.bas

Filenames are not required to be eight characters long, nor are extensions required to be three characters long. Those are only maximum limits.

Some software programs automatically attach extensions to the filenames assigned by the user to text and data files. For example, word processors often append a .DOC extension to documents created. The user does not even see the extension when files are listed from within these word processors. When an application program automatically backs up files, a .BAK extension is often added to revised text files.

Various spreadsheet programs automatically add file extensions to the worksheets created, including .WKS or .WK. Another common spreadsheet extension is .DIF, a standard devised by VisiCalc which enables spreadsheet files to be transferred from one spreadsheet program to another. When files are printed to disk rather than to a printer, a typical extension used is .PRN.

Data base managers often assign either .DB or .DBF for data base files.

In each case outlined above, the extension is automatically added by the software to keep files straight. These extensions are seldom seen within the software; only the first eight characters (i.e., characters prior to the delimiter) are displayed. The procedure allows the operator to name a worksheet as BUDGET and still generate a graph and perhaps a text file called BUDGET. The computer knows which is which because of the automatically generated different extensions. Respectively, the names might be BUDGET.WK, BUDGET.PIC, and BUDGET.PRN.

**DOS FILENAME EXTENSIONS**

DOS has its own set of extensions, many of which are used by specific software packages as mentioned above. The most common DOS assigned file extensions are:

| | |
|---|---|
| .BAK | for a DOS-created backup file |
| .BAS | for a BASIC language file |
| .BAT | for a batch processing file |
| .COM | for an external DOS command or program file |
| .EXE | for an executable program or command file |
| .HEX | for a file used with the Debug command |
| .MAP | for a file used with the Link command |
| .OBJ | for an object code file created by a compiler |
| .REL | for an object code file created by an assembler |
| .TMP | for a temporary file created by DOS |

As a side note, the .COM files on the DOS diskette are really special communication files. They correspond to the standard DOS external commands already discussed. Each .COM file contains raw machine language code (instructions). Whenever a DOS external command is entered (e.g., Chkdsk, Diskcopy, or Diskcomp), DOS immediately checks to see if there is a .COM file by that filename on the disk in the default or specified drive. If such a file is located, the machine language instructions contained in the file are loaded into memory and control of the system is passed to those instructions.

IMPORTANT NOTE: If no .COM file is found, then DOS checks first for an .EXE file, then for a .BAT file by the name entered. With these three types of extensions (.BAT, .COM, and .EXE), the extension is never entered, only the file specification.

## THE DRIVE DESIGNATION

In the earlier discussion of syntax, it was pointed out that Phil and Wayne needed to be told where to go to obtain a cola for Susan.

Similarly, DOS must know where commands are located, where files are stored and where specified actions are required. An IBM PC typically has one or two disk drives. Either the left-hand drive or the top drive (if the drives are stacked) is "drive A." The formal name is A: (the colon is a required part of the name, though in speaking we refer simply to "drive a").

If a second disk drive is included with the computer, it is referred to as "drive B." On an enhanced PC, IBM XT, or AT, the first hard-disk drive is referred to as drive c: or C:. Some computers may have additional drives labeled D:, E:, etc.

Back to the cola example, we might say "get a cola," but "go to the store and get a cola" is clearer. The computer needs similar clarification. If a program is to be loaded, is it on the disk in drive A: or B: or C: or D:? The drive designation accomplishes this task. It communicates to the computer where data is stored, should be stored, or on which drive commands to be executed are located.

## THE DEFAULT DRIVE

DOS makes life easy for the user. The DOS prompt will always display the default drive or the logged-on drive. The terms are synonymous. On a floppy drive system, after booting the computer with a diskette in drive a:, the DOS prompt will appear as:

    A>

On a hard-disk system, if booted with no disk in drive A:, the DOS prompt would appear as:

C>

What does this mean for the user?  A command or file may be accessed from the default drive without using the drive designation.  Two keystrokes are saved.

By simply typing in the drive designation (only) at the DOS prompt, we can change the default drive (also called the logged-on drive).

If logged-on to drive C:, the DOS prompt appears as:

C>

By typing B:  and pressing the ENTER key (also referred to as the RETURN key or <CR> for carriage return), the prompt switches to:

B>

## THE COMPLETE FILENAME

A completely assembled filename might appear as:

a:letter3.doc

This would be an appropriate filename for a letter created by a word processor using the .doc extension which is stored on drive A:.

In summary, the complete filename equals:

Drive Designation + File Specification + Extension

Even though the above represents the technical filename, most users consider the file specification as synonymous with the term **filename**.  The file on drive C:  called DOCUMENT with a .DOC extension is usually referred to as DOCUMENT, not A:DOCUMENT.DOC.

## WILDCARD CHARACTERS

Two characters are reserved for a special use and may not be used in the filename or extension.  These characters are the question mark (?) and the asterisk (*).

They are referred to as wildcard characters and may substitute for one or more characters in a filename. The question mark substitutes for one character; the asterisk may substitute for one or more characters.

Depending upon how we structure filenames, these wildcard characters may be very helpful. For example, it would be helpful when backing up specific files if we formed a habit of using common characters in files with common data.

Text files storing a group of letters might be named:

    LETTER1.DOC
    LETTER2.DOC
    LETTER3.DOC
    LETTER4.DOC

When backing up the files to disk, all of the LETTER files could be copied with one command rather than several. The DOS command Copy will duplicate the specified files. By using the ? wildcard, the following command would copy every file from drive A: to drive B: which began with LETTER and ended with a single character (any character, not just 1 through 9) which had the .DOC extension:

    COPY A:LETTER?.DOC B:

We will come back to wildcard characters in the Guided Activities. They are very handy little creatures. For now, remember that:

1. ? means any character may occupy that position in a filename.

2. * means any character may occupy that position and the remaining positions in the filename or extension.

3. These characters may not be used as part of the actual filename given a file.

## DISK HANDLING GUIDELINES

Whether working with DOS, an application program, or data diskettes; the handling of floppy disks is crucial. Diskettes are the tools of the computing trade. If you fail to properly handle these tools, trouble and inconvenience will follow.

Even if a computer includes a hard-disk system, you must work with floppy disks to **archive** application program disks, and to back up data. You cannot avoid working with diskettes--so learn how to use rather than abuse them.

Diskettes are composed of a jacket enclosing a thin circular piece of material. The disk might be compared to a phonograph record, except that it does not include physical groves or tracks--only electronic ones. The disk is coated with a magnetic oxide surface which holds small electrical charges representing the binary 0 and 1. These charges are then interpreted by the computer to represent characters of the alphabet, numbers and other special characters.

The surface of the diskette must be protected from any element or activity which might damage the surface.  Damage can occur by exposing the surface to contaminants (dust, dirt, fingerprints, liquids), physical damage (folding, creasing, bending, heavy objects, indentations from writing tools), heat (direct and prolonged sunlight, or temperatures above 122 degrees Fahrenheit), cold (below 50 degrees Fahrenheit), and magnetic fields (small motors, magnets, ringing telephones).

The jacket of each diskette has a window through which the disk drive read-write head accesses data.  The easiest method of damaging a diskette is to contaminate the magnetic oxide surface through that window.  Each diskette comes with a paper envelope.  To further protect the recording surface, the disk should always be housed in its jacket when not in use.  Refer to Figure 1-3 for a listing of important disk handling guidelines.

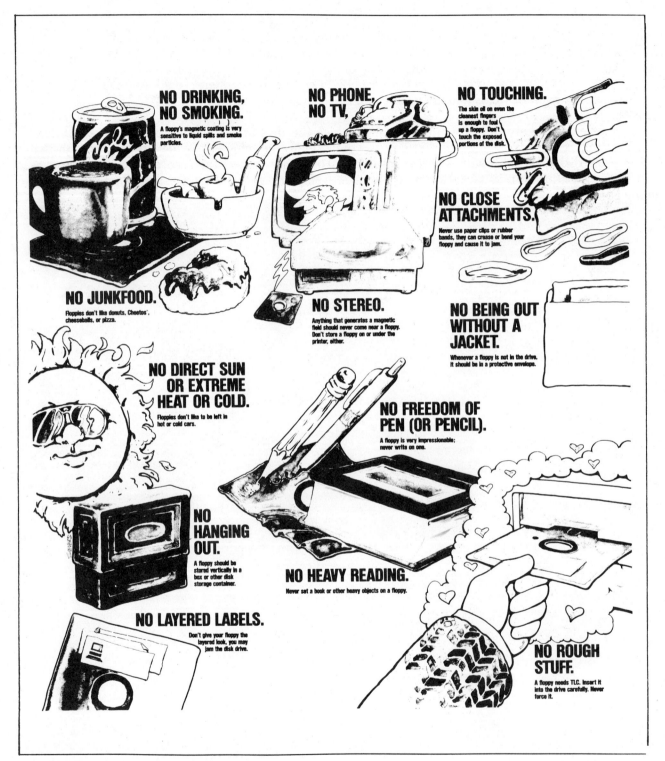

FIGURE 1-3.  Disk Handling Guidelines.

**REVIEW QUESTIONS**

1. What is the difference between the operating system on a mainframe and DOS on an IBM PC?

2. Define DOS.

3. Who developed IBM PC-DOS and MS-DOS?

4. What are the essential differences between PC-DOS and MS-DOS?

5. Where is IBM PC-DOS stored for use by the computer?

6. Can application programs (i.e., word processors, spreadsheets, and data managers) be run without DOS?

7. What was the significant new feature of DOS 2.0?

8. What was the significant new feature of DOS 3.0?

9. What was the significant new feature of DOS 3.2, and why was it not embraced by most computer users?

10. What is a syntax diagram?  Why is syntax important to a computer user?

11. When may internal and external DOS commands be executed?

12. What is the maximum number of characters which may be used in a file specification?  In an extension?

13. Which two keyboard characters may not be used when naming a file?  Why?

14. Which of the following are not legal filenames?

    LETTER\TO\MOTHER.TXT
    FINAL.LTR
    CALLHOME.DOC
    $%&9441!.BAK
    1.BAT
    COMMAND.COMM
    12345678.*90

15. How does the user change the default drive?

16. What is the difference between the default drive and the logged drive?

17. What is meant by case-sensitive?  Is DOS case-sensitive when naming a file or executing a DOS command?

18. Why is NEWSNOTE.DOC a better filename than &$123NTE.DOC?

## DOCUMENTATION RESEARCH

All Documentation Research within this text refers to the IBM DISK OPERATING SYSTEM Version 3.1 manual. Other versions of the manual may be used, but the chapter references will not apply. When using another version, scan the table of contents for topics similar to those suggested in the Documentation Research. For the following questions, read chapters 1 and 2 of the IBM DISK OPERATING SYSTEM version 3.1 manual.

1. What are the three types of diskettes supported by DOS 3.1? How much storage space, in kilobytes (K), does each provide?

2. What is drive compatibility? How does it affect the use of diskettes?

3. Which keyboard characters are invalid in a filename? Which are invalid in a file extension?

4. Give an example, using both wildcard characters, for which the result would be identical.

# 2 FUNDAMENTAL DOS COMMANDS

This second part of the text will cover the fundamental disk operating system commands. These commands are routinely used by microcomputer operators in the course of their daily and weekly work. Even if the user has an aversion to programming and the more complex types of computer tasks, these basic commands are essential.

The fundamental DOS commands fall into three groups: disk preparation commands, housekeeping commands and file management commands. Such tasks as preparing a disk for use; copying, deleting and renaming files; and comparing files and disks will be covered.

Throughout the guided activities in the remaining units, the authors have used certain conventions to assist in the step by step exercises. Whenever a single keystroke is required, the exercise will ask you to "Press" the designated key. Keys are indicated withing arrow brackets, i.e., you will be told to hit the tab key with the phrase Press <TAB>. <CR> is used throughout to indicate the need for a carriage return. To generate a <CR>, press the key marked either RETURN or ENTER. The exercises will ask you to "Type" when several keystrokes are required. Further, the words to type will be in boldface characters, i.e., Type **DOS** means press the letter D, then O followed by S.

# UNIT 2

# DISK PREPARATION COMMANDS

**SUPPLIES NEEDED**

The supplies that you will need for completing this unit are:

1. PC-DOS 3.10 program disk;
2. 5-1/4 inch double-sided, double-density diskette.

**OBJECTIVES**

After completing this unit, you will be able to:

1. explain the use of the Format command;
2. format a non-system diskette;
3. format a non-system diskette with a volume label;
4. format a system diskette;
5. format a non-system diskette on one side;
6. format an eight sector-per-track diskette;
7. format a double-sided non-system diskette in a high-capacity drive for use in a standard drive;
8. format a diskette for hidden DOS files;
9. format a one-sided system diskette with volume label;
10. transfer DOS files with Sys command;
11. format a system diskette;
12. create a duplicate diskette;
13. compare a newly created diskette with the original.

## IMPORTANT COMMANDS

The important commands introduced in this unit are:

1. Format command;
2. Sys command;
3. Diskcopy command;
4. Diskcomp command.


## ASSIGNMENTS

Place a check in front of the assignments for this unit:

1. ____ Review and understand the following term listed in Appendix A, the Computer Terms Dictionary: **initialization**.
2. ____ Guided Activity:  Format a Non-System Diskette.
3. ____ Guided Activity:  Format a Diskette with a Volume Label.
4. ____ Guided Activity:  Format a System Diskette.
5. ____ Guided Activity:  Format a System Diskette with a Volume Label.
6. ____ Guided Activity:  Format a One-Sided Diskette.
7. ____ Guided Activity:  Format a One-Sided Diskette with a Volume Label.
8. ____ Guided Activity:  Format an Eight-Sector Diskette.
9. ____ Guided Activity:  Format a Double-Sided Diskette in a High-Capacity Drive.
10. ____ Guided Activity:  Format a Diskette with Hidden DOS Files.
11. ____ Guided Activity:  Transfer the DOS System Files with Sys Command.
12. ____ Guided Activity:  Make a Duplicate Disk with the Diskcopy Command.
13. ____ Guided Activity:  Compare Two Diskettes with the Diskcomp Command.
14. ____ Answer the Review Questions.
15. ____ Documentation Research.


## DISK PREPARATION COMMANDS

The Format, Diskcopy, Diskcomp, and Sys commands are necessary commands to allow you to work and store data on your disks.


## GUIDED ACTIVITY:  LOADING DOS 3.10

1. Slowly insert the DOS diskette with the label up and toward you into disk drive A: and close the drive door.

2. If the PC is off, turn it on.  This activity will boot your computer system and load DOS.  DOS must be loaded before any computer activity can take place.  This method is called a cold start or cold boot.

3. If the PC is on, reset the system by holding down the CTRL and ALT keys, and simultaneously pressing the DEL key.  This method of booting is called a warm start or warm boot.

You will see the diskette drive light come on while DOS is being loaded, and you may hear some disk drive noise.  When DOS is loaded and ready, you will see the screen response:

    Current date is Tue 1-01-1980
    Enter new date (mm-dd-yy):_

When entering the new date, use the form MM/DD/YY, where MM = Month, DD = Day and YY = Year. In the example 8/21/86, "8" represents the month of August, "21" is the day of the month, and "86" represents the year 1986.

 4. Enter today's date.

 5. Press <CR>.

After entering the date, you can enter the time.  Time is displayed in hours, minutes, seconds, and hundredths of seconds. DOS displays the following screen response for entering time.

    Current time is 0:08:21.25
    Enter new time:_

DOS only understands time entered in 24-hour time.  By typing 18:30, you enter a time of 6:30 P.M.

 6. Enter current time.

 7. Press <CR>.

The last message you receive from DOS is:

    The IBM Personal Computer DOS
    Version 3.10 (C)Copyright International Business Machines Corp 1981, 1985
            (C)Copyright Microsoft Corp 1981, 1985
    A>_

## FORMAT COMMAND

The Format command is one of the most used DOS file commands.  Before you can use a diskette, whether it is a 5-1/4 inch floppy or a hard disk, you must prepare it to receive data.  Formatting a diskette creates a clean surface on the disk and removes all data.  It checks the disk surface for errors in construction and the suitability of the disk for receiving tracks and sectors.  When bad sectors are found on the disk surface, they are identified so that data will not be stored in these areas.  The directory that you view with the Dir command is created with the Format command.  Initializing, or formatting, creates a file allocation table (FAT) which allows you to see the file name, size, time, and date the files were created or last modified and stored on the disk.  After the disk is formatted, you can determine the number of usable bytes you have for storage and the number of bytes on the disk.

You can create different disk surfaces by using parameters or switches.  In the following examples, the "d:" after the Format command is the drive designator for the drive that contains the disk to be formatted.  Switches or parameters are composed of a slash (/) followed by one of several characters.

Be very careful when you use the Format command with a hard disk. If you do not identify a target drive with the Format command, it will format the current drive. In the case of a hard drive, that would be disastrous. All data would be removed from the hard disk drive.

COMMAND        ACTION

Format d:        format non-system 9-or-15 sector-per-track-diskette.

Format d:/V      format non-system diskette with a Volume Label.

Format d:/S      formats a diskette with the DOS operating system. This diskette then can be used to boot the system at start-up. This procedure places the system files IBMBIO.com, IBMDOS.com, and Command.com on the diskette.

Format d:/1      format non-system one-sided diskette.

Format d:/8      format non-system eight-sector-per-track disk.

Format d:/4      format non-system double-sided diskette in a high-capacity drive.

Format d:/B      format non-system diskette for eight sectors in order to leave space for the system files IBMBIO.com and IBMDOS.com, which can be copied to the diskette later.

**EVERYDAY FORMAT COMMAND SWITCHES**

In your work with the Format command, you will find some switches that you use more than others. The switches in this section are the ones that are most often needed in your everyday DOS work.

**GUIDED ACTIVITY: FORMAT A NON-SYSTEM DISKETTE**

The Format x: command (where x: designates the drive for the disk to be formatted) creates a formatted non-system diskette with DOS 3.1, using two floppy disk drives.

1. Place your DOS 3.1 diskette in drive A:

2. At the "A>" prompt, type **FORMAT B:**

3. Press <CR>.

4. Insert a new diskette in drive B:

5. Press <CR>.

6. If you do not want to format another disk, type **N**

7. Press <CR>.

If the diskette surface has any defects, DOS will not store data at those locations.  The number of bytes in bad sectors will be reported by DOS after formatting a diskette.

Figure 2-1 shows the screen response after formatting a diskette.

```
A>FORMAT B:
Insert new diskette for drive B:
and strike ENTER when ready

Formatting...Format complete

     362496 bytes total disk space
     362496 bytes available on disk

Format another (Y/N)? N
```

FIGURE 2-1.  Formatting a Non-System Diskette


**GUIDED ACTIVITY:  FORMAT NON-SYSTEM DISKETTE WITH VOLUME LABEL**

The Format x:/V command (where x: designates the drive for the disk to be formatted) creates a non-system diskette with a Volume label. The "/V" switch will allow you to place the Volume label "MEMO DISK" on the diskette.  If you use the Dir command with this disk, you will see the "MEMO DISK" label on the diskette.

1. Place your DOS 3.1 diskette in drive A:.

2. At the "A>_" type **FORMAT B:/V**

3. Press <CR>.

4. Insert a diskette in drive B: and Press <CR>.

5. When prompted for "Volume label," type **MEMO DISK**

6. Press <CR>.

7. If you do not want to Format another disk, type **N**

8. Press <CR>.

Figure 2-2 shows the screen results of formatting with volume label.

```
A>FORMAT B:/V
Insert new diskette for drive B:
and strike ENTER when ready

Formatting...Format complete
Volume label (11 characters, ENTER for none)? MEMO DISK


        362496 bytes total disk space
        362496 bytes available on disk

Format another (Y/N)?N
```

FIGURE 2-2.  Formatting with Volume Label

 9. Type **Dir B:**

10. Press <CR> to see the volume label.


**GUIDED ACTIVITY:  FORMATTING A SYSTEM DISKETTE**

The Format x:/S command (where x: designates the drive for the disk to be formatted) creates a self-booting system diskette.

 1. Place your DOS 3.1 diskette in drive A:.

 2. Type **Format B:/S**

 3. Press <CR>.

 4. Insert a diskette in drive B:.

 5. Press <CR>.

 6. If you do not want to format another disk, type **N**

 7. Press <CR>.

Figure 2-3 shows the screen response for formatting a system-bootable diskette.

```
A>FORMAT B:/S
Insert new diskette for drive B:
and strike ENTER when ready

Formatting...Format complete
System transferred


   362496 bytes total disk space
    62464 bytes used by system
   300032 bytes available on disk

Format another (Y/N)?N
```

FIGURE 2-3.  Formatting a System Diskette


**GUIDED ACTIVITY:  FORMAT SYSTEM DISKETTE WITH VOLUME LABEL**

1. Place your DOS 3.1 diskette in drive A:.

2. Type **FORMAT B:/S/V**

3. Press <CR>.

4. Insert a diskette in drive B:.

5. Press <CR>.

6. When prompted for "Volume Label," type **CLASS DISK**

7. Press <CR>.

8. If you do not want to format another disk, type **N**

9. Press <CR>.

Figure 2-4 shows the screen response for formatting a system diskette with a volume label.

```
A>FORMAT B:/S/V
Insert new diskette for drive B:
and strike ENTER when ready

Formatting...Format complete
System transferred

Volume label (11 characters, ENTER for none)? CLASS DISK

      362496 bytes total disk space
       62464 bytes used by system
      300032 bytes available on disk

Format another (Y/N)?N
```

FIGURE 2-4.  Formatting A System Diskette with Volume Label

10. Type **Dir B:**

11. Press <CR> and notice that the volume label is displayed on the screen along with the file Command.Com.

*Omit*

## INFREQUENTLY USED FORMAT COMMAND SWITCHES

The Format command and switches in this section will give you an opportunity to use and practice some of these infrequently used commands.

### GUIDED ACTIVITY:  FORMAT ONE-SIDED DISKETTE

The Format x:/1 command (where x: designates the drive for the disk to be formatted) creates a non-system one-sided diskette for data storage.

1. Place your DOS 3.1 diskette in drive A:.

2. At the "A>" prompt, type **FORMAT B:/1**

3. Press <CR>.

4. Insert a diskette in drive B:.

5. Press <CR>.

6. If you do not want to format another disk, type **N**

7. Press <CR>.

Figure 2-5 shows the screen response for formatting a one-sided diskette.

```
A>FORMAT B:/1
Insert new diskette for drive B:
and strike ENTER when ready

Formatting...Format complete

      179712 bytes total disk space
      179712 bytes available on disk

Format another (Y/N)?N
```

FIGURE 2-5.  Formatting a One-Sided Diskette

**GUIDED ACTIVITY:  FORMAT ONE-SIDED SYSTEM DISKETTE WITH VOLUME LABEL**

1. Place your DOS 3.1 diskette in drive A:.

2. Type **FORMAT B:/1/S/V**

3. Press <CR>.

4. Insert a diskette in drive B:.

5. Press <CR>.

6. Type **PLAY DISK**

7. Press <CR>.

8. If you do not want to format another disk, type **N**

9. Press <CR>.

Figure 2-6 shows the screen response for formatting a one-sided system diskette with label.

```
A>FORMAT B:/1/S/V
Insert new diskette for drive B:
and strike ENTER when ready

Formatting...Format complete
System transferred

Volume label (11 characters, ENTER for none)? PLAY DISK

        179712 bytes total disk space
         61440 bytes used by system
        118272 bytes available on disk

Format another (Y/N)?N
```

FIGURE 2-6.  Formatted One-Sided System Diskette with Label

10. Type **DIR B:**

11. Press <CR> and notice that the volume label is displayed on the screen along with the file Command.Com.

**GUIDED ACTIVITY:  FORMAT EIGHT-SECTOR DISKETTE**

The Format x:/8 command (where x: designates the drive for the disk to be formatted) creates an eight-sector rather than a nine-sector diskette.  DOS versions prior to DOS 2.0 must be formatted with eight sectors per track.

1. Place your DOS 3.1 diskette in drive A:.

2. Type **FORMAT B:/8**

3. Press <CR>.

4. Insert a diskette in drive B:.

5. Press <CR>.

6. If you do not want to Format another disk, type **N**

7. Press <CR>.

Figure 2-7 shows the screen response for formatting an eight-sector diskette.

```
A>FORMAT B:/8
Insert new diskette for drive B:
and strike ENTER when ready

Formatting...Format complete

      322560 bytes total disk space
      322560 bytes available on disk

Format another (Y/N)?N
```

FIGURE 2-7.  Formatting Eight-Sector Diskette

**GUIDED ACTIVITY:  FORMAT DOUBLE-SIDED DISKETTE IN HIGH-CAPACITY DRIVE**

The Format x:/4 command (where x: designates the drive for the disk to be formatted) creates a double-sided non-system diskette in a high-capacity disk drive, for the diskette to be used in a standard drive.  You will need access to a PC AT with a high-capacity drive to use this switch.

1. Place your DOS 3.1 diskette in drive A:

2. At the "A>" type **FORMAT A:/4**

3. Press <CR>.

4. Remove your DOS diskette from drive A: and place a new diskette in drive A:.

5. Press <CR>.

6. If you do not want to Format another disk, type **N**

7. Press <CR>.

Figure 2-8 shows the screen response when formatting a double-sided diskette in a high-capacity drive.

```
A>FORMAT A:/4
Insert new diskette for drive A:
and strike ENTER when ready

Formatting...Format complete

      362496 bytes total disk space
      362496 bytes available on disk

Format another (Y/N)?N
```

FIGURE 2-8.  Formatting Double-Sided Diskette

**GUIDED ACTIVITY:  FORMAT DISKETTE FOR HIDDEN FILES**

The Format x:/B command (where x: designates the drive for the disk to be formatted) creates space for the hidden DOS files on the formatted diskette.  The command will reserve the correct space on the diskette to allow you to add DOS system files on the diskette later.

1. Place your DOS 3.1 diskette in drive A:.

2. Type **FORMAT B:/B**

3. Press <CR>.

4. Insert a diskette in drive B:.

5. Press <CR>.

6. If you do not want to format another disk, type **N**

7. Press <CR>.

Figure 2-9 shows the screen response for formatting a diskette for hidden DOS files.

```
A>FORMAT B:/B
Insert new diskette for drive B:
and strike ENTER when ready

Formatting...Format complete

     322560 bytes total disk space
       9216 bytes used by system
     313344 bytes available on disk

Format another (Y/N)?N
```

FIGURE 2-9.  Formatting A Diskette for Hidden DOS Files

**SYS COMMAND**

The Sys command is used to copy the DOS hidden files from the DOS diskette.

**GUIDED ACTIVITY:  TRANSFERRING DOS SYSTEM FILES WITH SYS COMMAND**

1. Place your DOS 3.1 diskette in drive A:.

This procedure requires the use of a disk that has been formatted with the "/B" parameter or a program diskette that has been set to receive the hidden DOS files.  If later you want to make this diskette a self-booting system disk you will have to copy the DOS Command.com file to the diskette.  The Sys command copies only the hidden files to the diskette.

2. Type **SYS B:**

3. Press <CR>.

The screen response for the Sys command will be:

    A>SYS B:

    System transferred

4. Type **DIR B:**

5. Press <CR>.

Notice that no files are listed on the disk; only the two hidden files have been added to the disk in drive B:.

**DISKCOPY COMMAND**

The Diskcopy command is used to make copies of one disk onto another disk.

**GUIDED ACTIVITY:  MAKING A DUPLICATE DISK USING DISKCOPY COMMAND**

The Diskcopy command can be used to make a backup of a diskette.

1. Place your DOS diskette in drive A:.

2. Type **DISKCOPY A: B:**

3. Press <CR>.

4. Remove your DOS diskette from drive A: and Insert the disk you want to copy in drive A:.  If you want to make a copy of your DOS diskette, use it as your source diskette.

5. Insert your target diskette in drive B:. This is the diskette on which you want to make an exact duplicate from the original in drive A:.

6. Press <CR>.

7. If you do not want to diskcopy another disk, type **N**

Figure 2-10 shows the screen response for the Diskcopy command. On a previously formatted disk, you will not receive the message "Formatting while copying."

```
A>DISKCOPY A: B:

Insert SOURCE diskette in drive A:

Insert TARGET diskette in drive B:

Press any key when ready .  .  .

Copying 40 tracks
9 Sectors/Track, 2 Side(s)
Formatting while copying

Copy another diskette (Y/N)?N_
```

FIGURE 2-10.  Diskcopy Command

8. Type **DIR B:**

9. Press <CR> and notice that the DOS commands are now on the disk in drive B:.

## DISKCOMP COMMAND

The Diskcomp command is used to compare two diskettes. It lets you know if the duplicate diskette you made with Diskcopy is the same as the original. Diskcomp is only valid immediately after using the Diskcopy command. Diskcomp cannot be used with the Copy command.

**GUIDED ACTIVITY:  COMPARING TWO DISKETTES WITH DISKCOMP**

1. Place the DOS 3.1 diskette in drive A:.

2. Type **DISKCOMP A: B:**

3. Press <CR>.

4. Remove your DOS diskette from drive A:.

5. Insert the original diskette in drive A:.

6. Insert the duplicate diskette in drive B:.

7. Press <CR>.

8. If you do not want to Diskcomp another disk, type **N**

Figure 2-11 shows the screen response for the Diskcomp command.

```
A>DISKCOMP A: B:

Insert FIRST diskette in drive A:

Insert SECOND diskette in drive B:

Press any key when ready .  .  .

Comparing 40 tracks
9 sectors per track, 2 side(s)

Compare OK

Compare another diskette (Y/N) ?N
```

FIGURE 2-11.  Diskcomp Command

## COMMAND REVIEW DICTIONARY

In this unit, you have read about several DOS commands.  Most have optional parameters.  We have tried to cover both the common and the rarely used forms of each command.  The following forms of this unit's commands are the most frequently used and should be reviewed carefully.

FORMAT B:                    Creates a formatted non-system diskette.

FORMAT B:/S                  Creates a self-booting system diskette.

FORMAT B:/S/V                Creates a self-booting system diskette with a volume label.

DISKCOPY A: B:               Creates a duplicate diskette in drive B: of the diskette in drive A:.

DISKCOMP A: B:               Compares a copied diskette with the original.

## REVIEW QUESTIONS

1. When do you need to use the Format command with a "/S" switch?

2. What procedure would you follow to format a diskette with space for the DOS hidden files?

3. How many bytes are used to format a system diskette?

4. What procedure would you follow to make a duplicate diskette?

5. What procedure would you follow to verify a duplicate diskette was the same as the original?

## DOCUMENTATION RESEARCH

1. Research IBM DISK OPERATING SYSTEM Version 3.1 manual for DOS commands and parameters not used in class.

# UNIT

# 3

# THE HOUSEKEEPING COMMANDS

**SUPPLIES NEEDED**

The supplies that you will need for completing this unit are:

1. PC-DOS 3.1 program disk;
2. 5-1/4 inch double-sided, double-density diskette;
3. formatted 5-1/4 inch double-sided, double-density diskette with a "/S" parameter.

**OBJECTIVES**

After completing this unit, you will be able to:

1. use the Chkdsk command to determine total amount of disk space in bytes;
2. use the Chkdsk command to determine bytes available on a disk;
3. use the Chkdsk command to determine the amount of memory available in the computer;
4. use the Chkdsk command to determine the amount of memory used by the computer;
5. use the Chkdsk command with the "/V" parameter to view files and their paths on the disk you are checking;
6. use the Chkdsk command with the "/F" parameter to repair errors on your diskette.
7. use the Dir command to determine the date, time, and bytes used by a file;
8. use the Cls command to clear the monitor screen;
9. use the Prompt command to change the system prompt;
10. use the Date command to change or update the current date;
11. use the Time command to change or update the current time.

## IMPORTANT COMMANDS

The important commands introduced in this unit are:

1. Chkdsk command;
2. Directory command;
3. Cls command;
4. Prompt command;
5. Date command;
6. Time command.

## ASSIGNMENTS

Place a check in front of the assignments for this unit:

1. ____   Guided Activity:  Check a Diskette with the Chkdsk Command.
2. ____   Guided Activity:  Check a Diskette Using Chkdsk with the "/V" Parameter.
3. ____   Guided Activity:  Use the Dir Command to Scan a File.
4. ____   Guided Activity:  Use the Dir Command to Stop the Screen from Scrolling.
5. ____   Guided Activity:  Use the Dir Command to Produce Horizontal Filenames.
6. ____   Guided Activity:  Use the Dir Command with a Pause.
7. ____   Guided Activity:  Clear the Screen with the Cls Command.
8. ____   Guided Activity:  Use the Prompt Command to Change Your System Prompt.
9. ____   Guided Activity:  Use the Date Command to Change the Date.
10. ____   Guided Activity:  Use the Time Command to Change the System Time.
11. ____   Answer the Review Questions.
12. ____   Documentation Research.

## HOUSEKEEPING COMMANDS

"Housekeeping command" is the name given to a command that comes into play all the time.  Though you might not use the commands all the time, the results of these commands are felt every time you use DOS.  You will now learn the six housekeeping commands: Chkdsk, Directory, Cls, Prompt, Date, and Time.

## CHKDSK COMMAND

The Chkdsk command is used to check a disk's directories, files, and allocation table. It also tells you the total amount of disk space in bytes, bytes available, memory available, and memory used.

### GUIDED ACTIVITY:  USING THE CHKDSK COMMAND

1. Insert the DOS diskette in drive A: and shut the drive door.

2. Turn on the computer.

3. Enter the current date and time.

4. Place a DOS 3.1 formatted system disk into drive B: and shut the drive door.

5. Type **A:CHKDSK B:**

6. Press <CR>.

Figure 3-1 shows the screen response for the Chkdsk command. In this activity, the disk in drive B: was formatted with a "/S" parameter. Because you used this parameter, 38912 bytes are used for the hidden DOS files. The amount of total memory or bytes free may vary depending on the amount of memory in your computer.

```
A>CHKDSK B:
      362496 bytes total disk space
       38912 bytes in two hidden files
      235524 bytes in 1 user files
      300032 bytes available on disk

  458752 bytes total memory
  421888 bytes free
```

FIGURE 3-1.  Chkdsk Command

## GUIDED ACTIVITY:  USING CHKDSK WITH THE "/V" PARAMETER

The Chkdsk command with the "/V" parameter lets you view the files and their paths on the disk you are checking. If you look at the disk files using the "/V" parameter, you can see the DOS hidden files.

1. Type **A:CHKDSK B:/V**

2. Press <CR>.

Figure 3-2 shows the screen response for the Chkdsk "/V" command.

```
CHKDSK B:/V
Directory B:\
      B:\IBMBIO.COM
      B:\IBMDOS.COM
      B:\COMMAND.COM

   362496 bytes total disk space
    38912 bytes in 2 hidden files
    23552 bytes in 1 user files
   300032 bytes available on disk

   458752 bytes total memory
   421888 bytes free
```

FIGURE 3-2.  Chkdsk "/V" Command of Formatted Disk


**GUIDED ACTIVITY:  USING CHKDSK WITH THE "/F" PARAMETER**

The Chkdsk command with the "/F" parameter lets you repair errors in the directory or file allocation table on your diskettes.  If DOS finds errors on your diskette, DOS will respond with that information and give you the option of repairing the errors.

In the following example, you are going to check a disk that has been formatted with a "/S" parameter.

1. Type **A:CHKDSK B:/F**

2. Press <CR>.

Figure 3-3 shows the screen response for the Chkdsk "/F" command.

```
CHKDSK B:/F

        362496 bytes total disk space
         38912 bytes in 2 hidden files
         23552 bytes in 1 user files
        300032 bytes available on disk

        458752 bytes total memory
        421888 bytes free
```

FIGURE 3-3.  Chkdsk "/F" Command of Formatted Disk

## DIRECTORY COMMAND

The Dir command is used to view files on your disks.  When this command is used, the files on your disk are listed down the screen until all the files have been scanned by DOS.  Using the file Command.com as an example, the Dir command shows us the following file on the screen:

Example:

COMMAND COM   23120  3-07-85  1:43p

COMMAND is the file name.
COM is the file extension.
23120 bytes used.
3-07-85 is the date the file was created.
1:43 is the time the file was created.

## GUIDED ACTIVITY:  SCANNING A FILE

1. Place the DOS diskette in drive A:.

2. Type **DIR A:** to view the DOS files on drive A:.

3. Press <CR>.

You should see a list of DOS file names flow by on the screen.

**GUIDED ACTIVITY: STOPPING THE SCREEN FROM SCROLLING**

To stop the screen from scrolling, simultaneously press the CTRL key then the S key, then release.  The screen will stop and you can view these filenames.  To start the screen scrolling again, press any key.

  1. Type **DIR**

  2. Press <CR>.

  3. Press <CTRL S> to stop the screen from scrolling.

  4. Press <CR> to start the screen scrolling again.

**GUIDED ACTIVITY: HORIZONTAL FILENAMES**

The Dir command with the "/W" parameter will cause the filenames to appear horizontally across the screen.

  1. Type **DIR/W**

  2. Press <CR>.

Figure 3-4 shows the screen response for the Dir/W command.

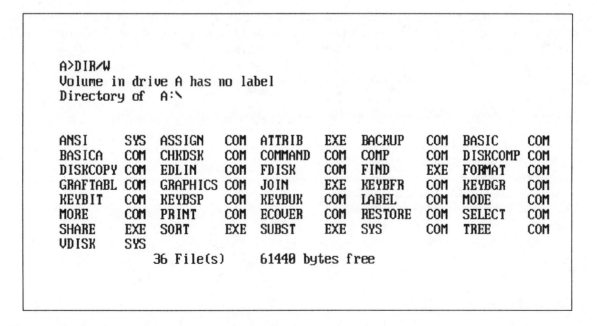

```
A>DIR/W
Volume in drive A has no label
Directory of  A:\


ANSI      SYS  ASSIGN   COM  ATTRIB   EXE  BACKUP   COM  BASIC    COM
BASICA    COM  CHKDSK   COM  COMMAND  COM  COMP     COM  DISKCOMP COM
DISKCOPY  COM  EDLIN    COM  FDISK    COM  FIND     EXE  FORMAT   COM
GRAFTABL  COM  GRAPHICS COM  JOIN     EXE  KEYBFR   COM  KEYBGR   COM
KEYBIT    COM  KEYBSP   COM  KEYBUK   COM  LABEL    COM  MODE     COM
MORE      COM  PRINT    COM  ECOVER   COM  RESTORE  COM  SELECT   COM
SHARE     EXE  SORT     EXE  SUBST    EXE  SYS      COM  TREE     COM
VDISK     SYS
            36 File(s)     61440 bytes free
```

FIGURE 3-4.  DIR/W Command

**GUIDED ACTIVITY:  DIR COMMAND WITH PAUSE**

The Dir command with a "/P" parameter will cause the screen to pause from scrolling after 23 files are on the screen.

1. Type **DIR/P**

2. Press <CR>.

The Dir/P command will cause the screen to scroll through 23 lines of text at one time.  Once 23 lines are displayed, the screen stops scrolling and waits for any key to be pressed before continuing.

3. Press <CR>.


**GUIDED ACTIVITY:  CLS COMMAND**

The Cls command is used to clear the screen of unwanted characters or text.

1. Type **ABCDEF** at A:

2. Press <CR>.

3. The screen will respond with:

   A>ABCDEF
   Bad command or file name

The letters "ABCDEF" are not a command or filename, so DOS gives the above message.

4. Type **CLS**

5. Press <CR>.

Now the only item on the screen will be the System prompt.


**PROMPT COMMAND**

The Prompt command is a fun and powerful tool for changing your DOS prompt. The simple command called Prompt, followed by text, can change the system prompt. If you typed **prompt HI!** and pressed the <Enter> key, you would be greeted with "HI!" on the screen.

There are special meta-strings that can be used with the Prompt text.  These characters are preceded by "$".  In our example above, if you wanted to have the drive identifier and ">" (greater-than sign) character following "HI!" you would type **HI! $n$g**. The $n is for the default drive and the $g is for the greater-than sign.

The following characters preceded by the dollar sign will cause the system prompt to produce the following on the screen:

$b   "|" vertical bar
$d   the DOS date
$e   escape character
$g   ">" greater-than-sign
$h   backspace
$l   "<" less-than-sign
$n   default drive
$p   directory of the default drive
$q   "=" equal sign
$t   DOS time
$v   DOS version number
$$   dollar sign
$_   underscore; causes the start of a new line


**GUIDED ACTIVITY:  CHANGING YOUR SYSTEM PROMPT**

The Prompt command can be used to change your DOS prompt and make some interesting greetings when you start your computer.

1. Type **PROMPT Hi!**

2. Press <CR>.

3. Type **PROMPT HI!  $n$g**

4. Press <CR>.

The screen response for the Prompt command is:

   HI! A>

5. Type **PROMPT** to return to the DOS system prompt.

6. Press <CR>.


**GUIDED ACTIVITY:  VIEWING YOUR DIRECTORY WITH SYSTEM PROMPT**

The Prompt command can be used to change your DOS prompt so you are able to determine the directory you are using.

1. Type **PROMPT $p$g**

2. Press <CR>.

The screen response for the Prompt command is A\ >, the backslash represents the root directory. With this command prompt, the current directory will always be shown in this position.

    A\ >_

3. Type **PROMPT** to return to the original DOS system prompt.

4. Press <CR>.


## DATE COMMAND

The Date command can be used either to enter the current date or to change the current system date. It is an internal DOS command that does not require the DOS diskette or DOS utility files to be resident in the default disk drive.

### GUIDED ACTIVITY:  CHANGING SYSTEM DATE

1. Type **DATE**

2. Press <CR>.

The screen response for the Date command is:

    A>DATE
    Current date is Thu  8-21-86
    Enter new date (mm-dd-yy):

In this example, you are going to enter the date May 1, 1986. The configuration for the Date command you are to enter is (mm-dd-yy) or (mm-dd-yyyy). The month (mm) can be entered as "05" or "5," day (dd) can be entered as "01" or "1," and the year (yy), (yyyy) can be entered as a two or four digit number:(in the example, the year could be "1986" or just"86"). You may use a period, slash, or hyphen to separate the date numbers.

3. Type **01.01.1986**

4. Press <CR>.

5. Type **DATE**

6. Press <CR>.

Let's enter an incorrect date and see DOS's response!

7. Type **13-25-79**

8. Press <CR>.

DOS will respond with "invalid date," and request you to enter a new date. There were two errors in the above date entry. The first is obvious; there are only 12 months in a year, so 13 is not correct. The second error was not so obvious as the first.  DOS will allow us to enter years only from 1980 through 1999.  The year 1979 was incorrect, and DOS responded with an invalid message.

 9. Type **01/25/99**

10. Press <CR>.

11. Type **DATE**

12. Press <CR>.

13. Enter today's date.

14. Press <CR>.


## TIME COMMAND

The Time command will allow you to enter or change the system time that you want to appear on your file directories on your diskettes.

## GUIDED ACTIVITY:  CHANGING SYSTEM TIME

 1. Type **TIME**

 2. Press <CR>.

DOS will respond with the current time and ask you to enter a new time.  For example, the time 6:00 P.M. would be entered as 18:00.  Remember to separate the hours and minutes with a colon.

 3. Enter the current time.

 4. Press <CR>.

**COMMAND REVIEW DICTIONARY**

In this unit, you have read about several DOS commands. Most have optional parameters. We have tried to cover both the common and the rarely used forms of each command. The following forms of this unit's commands are the most frequently used and should be reviewed carefully.

| | |
|---|---|
| CHKDSK B: | Checks the general condition of the diskette. |
| CHKDSK B:/F | Checks the diskette and allows you to correct errors. |
| DIR | Lists files on the current disk drive. |
| DIR/P | Causes the screen to stop scrolling after 23 files are viewed. |
| DATE | Allows you to enter or change the current date. |
| TIME | Allows you to enter or change the current time. |

**REVIEW QUESTIONS**

1. How would you view the hidden DOS files?

2. What procedure would you follow to determine the amount of memory available in your computer?

3. What command will tell you when a file was created or last used?

4. What command will allow you to view your diskette files and directory paths?

5. What command will clear your monitor of unwanted characters?

6. What command will tell you if you have bad bytes on your disk?

**DOCUMENTATION RESEARCH**

1. Research IBM DISK OPERATING SYSTEM Version 3.1 manual for DOS information about diskette construction.

# UNIT

# 4 FILE MANAGEMENT COMMANDS

**SUPPLIES NEEDED**

The supplies that you will need for completing this unit are:

1. PC-DOS 3.10 program disk;
2. two formatted 5-1/4 inch double-sided, double-density diskettes.

**OBJECTIVES**

After completing this unit, you will be able to:

1. use the Copy command to copy files to your screen;
2. use the Copy command to copy files to your printer;
3. use the Copy command to copy files to other disk drives;
4. create a file using the Copy command;
5. copy files using wildcard characters;
6. combine files to form one file;
7. use the Comp command to compare files;
8. use the Rename command to change the name of a file;
9. use the Delete command to delete files.

## IMPORTANT COMMANDS

The important commands introduced in this unit are:
 1. Copy command;
 2. Comp command;
 3. Delete command;
 4. Rename command.

## ASSIGNMENTS

Place a check in front of the assignments for this unit:

1. ____ Review and understand the following terms listed in Appendix A in the Computer Terms Dictionary: **End-of-File Mark, Wildcard, Internal Command, External Command.**
2. ____ Guided Activity:  Copy a File Using the Copy Command.
3. ____ Guided Activity:  Copy a File to the Screen.
4. ____ Guided Activity:  Copy a File to Another Drive.
5. ____ Guided Activity:  Copy a File with Wildcard Characters.
6. ____ Guided Activity:  Combine Two Files.
7. ____ Guided Activity:  Copy a File to Your Printer.
8. ____ Guided Activity:  Compare Two Files with the Comp Command.
9. ____ Guided Activity:  Rename a File.
10. ____ Guided Activity:  Delete a Group of Files with Wildcard Characters.
11. ____ Answer the Review Questions.
12. ____ Documentation Research.

## FILE MANAGEMENT COMMANDS

File Management commands will help you manage the files on your floppy and hard disks.  These commands are internal DOS commands and do not require you to have your DOS diskette resident in your disk drives after you have loaded DOS into memory.

Managing your disks will require you to copy, delete, rename, and compare files within your disks and directories.  The commands that will accomplish these tasks and that will be covered in this unit, are: Copy, Comp, Delete, and Rename.

## GUIDED ACTIVITY:  STARTING THE COMPUTER

 1. Insert the DOS 3.1 program diskette in drive A: and shut the drive door.

 2. Turn on the computer.

 3. Enter the current date and time.

 4. Remove your DOS diskette from drive A:.

 5. Place a formatted 5-1/4 disk in drive A:.

6. Place a formatted 5-1/4 disk in drive B:.


## COPY COMMAND

The Copy command is an **internal** DOS command used to copy a file or files to a disk from another disk or directory. The Copy command will also copy input from your keyboard and display that input to your monitor and printer.


### GUIDED ACTIVITY:  CREATING A FILE USING THE COPY COMMAND

You can create a file directly from your keyboard with the COPY command.  When you do this, you must tell DOS the file is being input from the keyboard.  You accomplish this by typing the word CON after the command Copy and before the filename.  If you want to create a file called **CLASS1.LST**, the command would be **COPY CON CLASS1.LST**.  If you want the file to be stored on a drive other than the default drive, use a drive identifier in the command syntax after the word **CON**.  The command to store the file on drive B: would look like this:  **COPY CON B:CLASS1.LST**.  This procedure creates an ASCII text file which you will be able to copy from disk to disk, see on your screen, and print on your printer.

When you are typing in COPY CON, you can only make corrections on the current line.  If you find you have made a mistake and wish to cancel the file, press CTRL C.

1. Type **COPY CON CLASS1.LST**

2. Press <CR>.

3. Type **Dean Swenson**

4. Press <CR>.

5. Type **Bill Richards**

6. Press <CR>.

7. Type **Hank Miller**

8. Press <CR>.

When you press <CTRL Z> or press function key <F6>, a special character is placed at the end of the file.  When DOS comes to the end of your file, it will know the file is finished because of this character.  The character is called **"End-of-file mark."**

9. Press <CTRL Z>.

10. Press <CR>.

The screen will respond with:

1 File(s) copied

## GUIDED ACTIVITY:  COPYING A FILE TO THE SCREEN

You can use the Copy command to copy the contents of a file to the screen.  To see the results of the last activity, we again use COPY CON, but this time we place CON after the filename in your command. The command syntax is COPY CLASS1.LST CON.

1. Type **COPY CLASS1.LST CON**

2. Press <CR>.

The screen response for the COPY CLASS1.LST CON command will be:

    A>CLASS1.LST CON
    Dean Swenson
    Bill Richards
    Hank Miller
            1 File(s) copied

## GUIDED ACTIVITY:  COPY A FILE TO ANOTHER DRIVE

In this activity you are going to copy the file named CLASS1.LST from drive A:, our source drive, to drive B:, our target drive.  In order to assure that the file is copied correctly, you are going to use the "/V" parameter with the COPY command.  This parameter will check that the sectors copied to the new drive are correct and the file is intact.  The command syntax to COPY a file with the "/V" parameter to another drive is: COPY A:CLASS1.LST B:/V.  This command will copy the file CLASS1.LST from drive A: to drive B: and verify that the file was copied correctly.

1. Type **COPY A:CLASS1.LST B:/V**

2. Press <CR>.

3. Type  **DIR B:**

4. Press <CR> to view the file on drive B:.

## GUIDED ACTIVITY:  CREATE ANOTHER FILE

This time you will save the copied file directly to drive B: rather than drive A:.  Notice how the syntax changes in this procedure.

1. Type **COPY CON B:CLASS2.LST**

2. Press <CR>.

3. Type **Joe Pine**

4. Press <CR>.

5. Type **Mary Paul**

6. Press <CR>.

7. Type **Susan Donald**

8. Press <CR>.

9. Press <CTRL Z>.

10. Press <CR>.

11. Type **DIR B:**

12. Press <CR>.

Figure 4-1 shows the files on drive B:.

```
A>DIR B:

Volume in drive B has no label
Directory of  B:\

CLASS1    LST       42  10-25-86    5:35a
CLASS2    LST       35  10-25-86    5:41a


    2 File(s)     360448 bytes free
```

FIGURE 4-1.  Dir of Drive B:

**GUIDED ACTIVITY:  COPYING FILES WITH WILDCARD CHARACTER**

You can use **wildcard** characters to copy files to another disk or directory. The * is a wildcard which can be used to copy both the files on drive B: to drive A:.  In our example, both files have the same extension LST, but different filenames.  We can substitute the wildcard * in place of the their filenames and type only the extension.  The syntax would look like this: COPY B:*.LST A:.

1. Type **COPY B:*.LST A:**

2. Press <CR>.

Use the DIR command to view the files on drive A:.


**GUIDED ACTIVITY:  COPY A FILE TO THE SAME DRIVE AND DIRECTORY**

DOS will not allow you to copy a file to the same disk directory in which the file resides.  If you want to do this you must give the file a different name.  You are going to give the file called CLASS1.LST a new name while using the Copy command in this activity.

1. Type **COPY CLASS1.LST CLASS3.LST**

2. Press <CR>.

3. Type **DIR**

4. Press <CR>.

Figure 4-2 shows the result of the Copy command used to copy a file to the same drive and directory. You now have two files that are the same, in the same place, but with different names.

```
A>DIR

Volume in drive A has no label
Directory of A:\

CLASS1     LST         42   10-25-86     5:35p
CLASS2     LST         35   10-25-86     5.41p
CLASS3     LST         42   10-25-86     5:35p
                 3 File(s)    359424    bytes free
```

FIGURE 4-2.  Copy and Change Name of File

**GUIDED ACTIVITY:  COPYING MORE FILES WITH WILDCARDS**

The question mark (?) in your example takes the place of the last character in your filename.  When you request the Copy command to copy the files in the example, it reads the files as if they were all the same and copies them.

1. Type **COPY CLASS?.\* B:**

2. Press <CR>.

The screen response to your command will be:

```
A>COPY CLASS?.*  B:
CLASS1.LST
CLASS2.LST
CLASS3.LST
        3 File(s)copied
```

**GUIDED ACTIVITY:  COPYING WITH \*.\***

In this activity you will copy the files with the wildcard characters in both the name and extension.

1. Type **COPY \*.\* B:**

2. Press <CR>.

The screen displays the fast method of copying files using global wildcard characters.

```
A>COPY *.* B:
CLASS1.LST
CLASS2.LST
CLASS3.LST
        3 File(s)copied
```

**GUIDED ACTIVITY:  COMBINING FILES**

The Copy command will allow you to combine files.  The files are combined by placing a plus sign between the files and then giving a new filename for the combined file.  The command syntax to combine the files CLASS1.LST and CLASS2.LST would be COPY CLASS1.LST+CLASS2.LST TOTCLASS.ROS.

1. Type **COPY CLASS1.LST+CLASS2.LST TOTCLASS.ROS**

2. Press <CR>.

The screen response shows the combining of the two files.

```
A>COPY CLASS1.LST+CLASS2.LST TOTCLASS.ROS
CLASS1.LST
CLASS2.LST
        1 File(s)copied
```

Use the Dir command to view the file TOTCLASS.ROS on drive A:

**GUIDED ACTIVITY:  COPYING A FILE TO PRINTER**

The Copy command will allow you to copy the contents of a file to the printer.  The command COPY TOTCLASS.ROS PRN will copy the contents of the file TOTCLASS.ROS to the printer PRN.

1. Turn on your printer.

2. Type **COPY TOTCLASS.ROS PRN**

3. Press <CR>.

The screen response for the command will be:

A>COPY TOTCLASS.ROS PRN
      1 File(s) copied

The output to your printer will list all the names which have been combined into the one file.

Dean Swenson
Bill Richards
Hank Miller
Joe Pine
Marry Paul
Susan Donald

## COMP COMMAND

The Comp command is used to compare the contents of a file, or a group of files, to a like file, or group of files. You use the Comp command after the Copy command to ensure that the files you copied compare OK.

## GUIDED ACTIVITY:  COMPARING FILES WITH COMP COMMAND

The Comp command is an **external** DOS command, and will require that the DOS diskette be resident in the computer to start the command. When you give the command Comp, your computer will ask you to "Enter the primary file name"; after you do this, it will ask you to "Enter the 2nd file name or drive id." The command will not remind you to do any disk swapping, so remember to change your disks if required to compare your files.

In your exercise, you are going to compare the files you created with COPY CON. When these files have been compared, you receive a message "Eof mark not found." The "End of file mark" is placed at the end of a file by pressing <CTRL Z> or <F6>. The "End of file mark" tells DOS the file is finished. In this example, as long as your files compare ok, they are correct. If you were comparing program files which often contain "Eof mark" and received the message, "Eof file mark not found," you could have cause for concern.

1. Place your DOS diskette in drive A:.

2. Type **COMP A:CLASS1.LST**

3. Press <CR>.

4. Remove your DOS diskette from drive A:.

5. Place the disk which contains the file CLASS1.LST in drive A:.

6. Type **B:CLASS1.LST**

7. Press <CR>.

8. Type **N**

Figure 4-3 shows the screen response for the Comp command.

```
A>COMP A:CLASS1.LST

Enter 2nd file name or drive id
B:CLASS1.LST

A:CLASS1.LST and B:CLASS1.LST

Eof mark not found

Files compare ok

Compare more files (Y/N)? N
```

FIGURE 4-3.  Comp Command

**RENAME COMMAND**

The Rename (Ren) command is an internal DOS command which does not require the DOS disk to be resident in the computer. The REN command allows you to change the name of your file.  As you saw in the Copy command, changing a filename allows you to copy the file to the same drive and directory.

**GUIDED ACTIVITY:  CHANGING A FILE NAME**

To change the name of a file, you first type the name of the command, followed by the drive name, old file name, then the new file name.  To rename the file CLASS1.LST to OFFICE.LST on disk drive A:, type **REN A:CLASS1.LST OFFICE.LST**.  Whenever you are working within the same drive and directory, you may omit the drive name.  The command would look like the this: REN CLASS1.LST OFFICE.LST.  When you invoke the command, the only response will be that the drive light will come on when the new name is written to the disk.

1. Type **REN A:CLASS1.LST OFFICE.LST**

2. Press <CR>.

Use the Dir command to see the filename change of your file.

3. Type **REN CLASS2.LST HOME.LST**

4. Press <CR>.

5. Type **DIR**

6. Press <CR>.

Figure 4-4 shows the change you made with the Ren command.

```
DIR

Volume in drive A has no label
Directory of A:\

OFFICE    LST     42    10-26-86    12:06a
HOME      LST     35    10-26-86    12:11a
CLASS3    LST     42    10-26-86    12:06a
          3 File (s)   320512 bytes free
```

FIGURE 4-4.  Rename Command


**DELETE/ERASE COMMAND**

The Delete and the Erase command both erase files from disks. It does not matter which command you use, they both do the same thing. The advantage of the Delete command is that it requires fewer characters to be typed in the command name. To delete a file, you type Del and specify where the file is that will be deleted.

Since the Delete command removes files from your disks, you should be careful with the command. It will allow you to use global wildcards like the copy command, and also gives you the ability to delete one or more files at a time.

**GUIDED ACTIVITY:  DELETING A SINGLE FILE FROM THE CURRENT DRIVE**

When you invoke the Del command, you won't see the changes until you look at the directory of the disk. Again, the only visible response to the command will be that the drive light will momentarily come on while the file is being deleted.

1. Type **DEL A:CLASS3.LST**

2. Press <CR>.

Use the Dir command to view the files on drive A:.

**GUIDED ACTIVITY:  USING WILDCARD CHARACTERS WITH THE DEL COMMAND**

The Del command will allow the substitution of wildcard characters in the command line.  In the following example, if you invoke the command DEL OFFICE.*, you will delete the file OFFICE.LST.  If you invoke the command DEL *.LST, you will delete all the files.  When the command says "delete the file with the extension LST" since both files have the extension, both files will be deleted.

1. Type **DEL *.LST**

2. Press <CR>.

Use the Dir command to view the the directory of the disk in drive A:.

3. Type **DEL B:*.***

4. Press <CR>.

DOS responds with the message, "Are you sure (Y/N)?_".  If you type **Y** for yes and press <CR>, all the files on the disk in drive B: will be deleted.

5. Type **Y**

6. Press <CR>.

Use the Dir command to view the the directory of the disk in drive B:.

## COMMAND REVIEW DICTIONARY

In this unit,you have read about several DOS commands.  Most have optional parameters.  We have tried to cover both the common and the rarely used forms of each command.  The following forms of this unit's commands are the most frequently used and should be reviewed carefully.

COPY A:Example.txt B:          Copies the file Example.txt in drive A: to drive B:

COPY A:Example.txt b:/V        Copies and verifies the file was copied correctly.

COPY *.* B:                    Copies all files in resident drive to drive B:.

COMP A:*.* C:                  Compares all files on drive A: with files with the same names on drive C:.

REN A:Joe.txt Bill.txt         Renames the file Joe.txt in drive A: to Bill.txt.

DEL A:Example.txt              Deletes the file Example.txt in drive A:.

DEL B:Example.txt              Deletes the file Example.txt in drive B:.

DEL A:*.*                      Deletes all files in drive A:.

## REVIEW QUESTIONS

1. What command sequence would you use to create a file?

2. How would you copy a file to your printer?

3. How would you create a backup file on the same disk and directory?

4. How would you combine two files?

5. How would you copy all the files on a disk to another disk with one command?

6. How would you delete all the files on a disk with one command?

# APPLICATION

**PART 1:  BUILDING A FILE WITH COPY CON**

In the previous unit we used Copy Con to build a text file.  In this application, you will build a file with Copy Con and save it on a 5 1/4 inch floppy disk.

A. Create a text file called Address.

B. In the text file place your name, street address, city, state, zip code, and date of birth; each on a separate line.

C. Turn the disk in to your instructor.

# PART

# 3

# INTERMEDIATE AND ADVANCED DOS COMMANDS

This third and final part of the text will cover DOS commands for the intermediate and advanced user. Each of the commands goes beyond the needs of the novice user who is only concerned with using application files, formatting disks and storing data files.

In the following units you will experiment with the DOS line editor, Edlin, and create batch files to accomplish tasks which normally require keyboard execution of several DOS commands. You will look at hard disk management and how organizing the storage of 25-50 diskettes of data, on one hard disk, can be made easier.

The text will explore the concept of disaster recovery plans and the DOS commands used to safeguard data. Additional advanced DOS programming concepts will be explored which allow redirection of input and output, background printing, and creating virtual disks.

The text will examine new computing concepts for the microcomputer including networking, file sharing, DOS shells and conclude with an examination of the future directions DOS development may take.

UNIT

# 5

# THE EDITING DOS COMMANDS

**SUPPLIES NEEDED**

The supplies that you will need for completing this unit are:

1. PC-DOS 3.10 program disk;
2. 5-1/4 inch formatted, double-sided, double-density diskette.

**OBJECTIVES**

After completing this unit, you will be able to:

1. write a text file;
2. edit a text file;
3. search and replace words within the text file;
4. move text to other lines within the text file;
5. print the text file to the screen.

## IMPORTANT COMMANDS

The important commands introduced in this unit are:

1. Edlin command;
2. Insert command;
3. List command;
4. Ending command;
5. Type command;
6. Delete command;
7. Abort command;
8. Edit command;
9. Copy command;
10. Move command;
11. Search command;
12. Replace command.

## ASSIGNMENTS

Place a check in front of the assignments for this unit:

1. ____ Guided Activity:  Write an eight-line text file using Edlin.
2. ____ Guided Activity:  Print the text file on a printer.
3. ____ Guided Activity:  Print the text file to your screen.
4. ____ Answer the Review Questions.

## EDLIN--THE TEXT EDITOR

Edlin is a text editor provided with your copy of PC/MS-DOS.  You can use it to generate text files.  It works with one line at a time and is very useful in the creation of batch files.  It will allow you to search and replace text, move lines, and copy lines. However, it is very limited as a word processor.

## GUIDED ACTIVITY:  STARTING EDLIN

1. Place a DOS 3.1 disk in drive A:.

2. Place a formatted disk in drive B:.

3. Turn on your computer.

4. Enter the current date and time.

Edlin is an external DOS file which is used as a text editor.  You will need the Edlin.Com file in order to use Edlin to write a text file.  By typing **EDLIN B:SCREEN.TXT** at the A: system prompt, you begin a new Edlin file named Screen.txt and the file will be written to drive B: when it is stored.

5. Type **EDLIN B:SCREEN.TXT**

6. Press <CR>.

When you start a new file, Edlin will state this at the beginning of the file.

The screen will show the new Edlin file Screen.txt:

    A>EDLIN B:SCREEN.TXT
    New file
    *
    _

**GUIDED ACTIVITY:  INSERT COMMAND**

When you start a new Edlin file, you must use the "I," insert line command.  The first line of the text file must be inserted using the Insert command.  Edlin automatically gives each line of text a line number when you press the <carriage return>.  Later, you will see that these line numbers make it easier to edit the Edlin file.

1. Type **I**

2. Press <CR>.

The screen response for "I" is:

    A>EDLIN B:SCREEN.TXT
    New file
    *I

            1:*_

The asterisk is the system prompt used by Edlin.  All Edlin commands start at the prompt.  This is the starting point for your new file Screen.txt.  Edlin will allow you to type 253 characters on a line, but will not hyphenate the words when it moves to the next line.

3. Type **B & C OFFICE HELP SCREEN.**

4. Press <CR>.

Figure 5.1 shows the screen response for inserting line 1.

```
A>EDLIN B:SCREEN.TXT
New file
*I

        1:* B & C OFFICE HELP SCREEN.
        2:*_
```

FIGURE 5-1.  Insert Command Line 1

5. You are now ready to enter more lines in your file.  You are going to leave a blank line after line 1. All you need to do to accomplish this is to enter a <carrage return> for line 2.

6. Press <CR>.

Figure 5-2 shows the screen response for inserting a blank line at Line 2.

```
A>EDLIN B:SCREEN.TXT
New file
*I

        1:* B & C OFFICE HELP SCREEN
        2:*
        3:*_
```

FIGURE 5-2.  Line 2

You are now ready to enter line 3.  Remember, when you start typing, the words will appear on the numbered line 3.

7. Type **Place your Wordprocessing Program disk in drive A:.**

8. Press <CR>.

Figure 5-3 shows the screen response for line 3.

```
A>EDLIN B:SCREEN.TXT
New file
*I

        1:* B & C OFFICE HELP SCREEN
        2:*
        3:* Place your Wordprocessing Program Disk in Drive A:.
        4:*_
```

FIGURE 5-3.  Line 3

**GUIDED ACTIVITY:  INSERT A LINE INTO AN EXISTING FILE**

1. Press <CTRL C> to stop inserting lines.

Figure 5-4 shows the screen response for stopping the Insert operation.

```
A>EDLIN B:SCREEN.TXT
New file
*I

        1:* B & C OFFICE HELP SCREEN.
        2:*
        3:* Place your Wordprocessing Program Disk in drive A:.
        4:*^C

*_
```

FIGURE 5-4.  Stop Inserting

Now you can insert new lines into your file.  The first line will be at the beginning of your file, at line 1. When you insert new lines into the existing file, all lines will move forward and be renumbered automatically, although you will not see the renumbered lines until you use the List command to list the line in the file.

 2. Type 1I

 3. Press <CR>.

The screen response for the 1I command is:

    *1I

            1:*_

 4. Type GOOD MORNING.

 5. Press <CR>.

To retain the blank line at line 2, you need to place a carriage return at that line.

 6. Press <CR>.

 7. Press <CTRL C> to stop the insert function.

Figure 5-5 shows the screen response for new line 1 and the carriage return in line 2.

```
*1I

     1:*GOOD MORNING.
     2:*
     3:*^C

*_
```

FIGURE 5-5.  New Line 1


## GUIDED ACTIVITY:  LIST LINES

The List command is used to display lines within your file.  You have the ability to list a single line or a group of lines.  The command is very straightforward.  To list line 1, type **1,1L** and press the <carriage return>.  If you type the command 1L and press the <carriage return>, you will list 23 lines starting with line 1.  To list a group of lines between lines 1 and 3, you type **1,3L** and press the <carriage return>.

1. Type **1L**

2. Press <CR>.

Figure 5-6 shows the screen response to the List command.

```
      *1L

            1:GOOD MORNING.
            2:
            3:*B & C OFFICE HELP SCREEN.
            4:
            5:Place your Wordprocessing Program disk in drive A:.
      *_
```

FIGURE 5-6.  List Command

If you wanted to list only lines 3 through 5, you would enter the command 3,5L.

3. Type **3,5L**

4. Press <CR>.

Figure 5-7 shows the screen response for List command 3,5L.

```
*3,5L
          3:*B & C OFFICE HELP SCREEN.
          4:
          5:Place your Wordprocessing Program disk in drive A:.
*_
```

FIGURE 5-7.  3,5L List Command


## GUIDED ACTIVITY:  ENDING AND SAVING EDLIN TEXT FILE

To end Edlin and save your file, you must type the letter "E" at the asterisk prompt and press the carriage return.

1. Type **E**

2. Press <CR>.


## TYPE COMMAND

The Type command displays the contents of a file on the computer screen.  It will display to the screen exactly what is in the file.  The command is similar to Copy Con and, like it, can be used to print to the printer if you use the extension >PRN at the end of the command line.

The command syntax for the Type command is straightforward.  Use the command name, tell DOS where the file is, and list the filename.  The command TYPE B:SCREEN.TXT will cause DOS to look to drive B: for the file Screen.txt and display it on the screen.


## GUIDED ACTIVITY:  PRINT TO SCREEN WITH TYPE COMMAND

1. Type **CLS** to clear your screen of data.

2. Press <CR>.

3. Type **TYPE B:SCREEN.TXT**

4. Press <CR>.

Figure 5-8 shows the Print To Screen response.

```
A>Type B:SCREEN.TXT
GOOD MORNING.

B & C OFFICE HELP SCREEN.

Place your Wordprocessing program disk in Drive A:.

A>_
```

FIGURE 5-8.  Screen Print

## GUIDED ACTIVITY:  DELETE AND ABORT COMMANDS

You are now going to leave your first file, Screen.txt; create a new file called Screen.ttt, and practice the Delete and Abort commands.

 1. Type **EDLIN SCREEN.TTT**

 2. Press <CR>.

The screen shows a new Edlin file, Screen.ttt.

```
A>EDLIN SCREEN.TTT
New file
*
 _
```

3. Type **1I**

4. Press <CR>.

5. Type **It has been a good day.**

6. Press <CR>

7. Type **Pack up your computer.**

8. Press <CR>.

9. Type **Good Night.**

10. Press <CR>.

11. Type **Bye.**

12. Press <CR>.

13. Press <CTRL C>.

Let's take a quick look at your new file.

14. Type **1L**

15. Press <CR>.

Figure 5-9 shows the screen response for the 1L List command.

```
*1L

        1:It has been a good day.
        2:Pack up your computer.
        3:Good Night.
        4:Bye.
```

FIGURE 5-9.  1L Command of New File Screen.TTT

To delete line 1, you only have to type **1D** for the line to be deleted.  If you wanted to delete a group of lines, you would type the beginning line followed by a comma, then the last line, and press <carriage return>.

16. Type **1D** to delete line 1.

17. Press <CR>.

18. Type **1L** to see the list.

19. Press <CR>.

Figure 5-10 shows the screen response for deleting and listing line 1.

```
*1L
        1:*Pack up your computer.
        2:Good Night.
        3:Bye.
```

FIGURE 5-10.  Delete Command

20. Type **1,3D** to delete lines 1 through 3.

21. Press <CR>.

22. Type **1L**

23. Press <CR>.

The screen shows the results of the 1,3D command.  All the lines have been deleted from the file and you are left with just the Edlin system prompt.

       *
       _

Any time you want to stop Edlin, you can use the Abort command.  It must be used at the Edlin asterisk prompt.  You simply type the letter "Q" at the prompt, press the <carriage return>, and follow the instructions.

24. Type **Q**

25. Press <CR>.

Edlin will ask you if you want to abort this file.  If you respond with **Y**, the file will be aborted and will not be saved.

26. Type **Y**

The screen response for the Abort command is:

    *Q
    Abort edit (Y/N) ?Y_

    A>_


## GUIDED ACTIVITY:  INSERT COMMAND

After your file has been created, there are times when you will want to add or insert lines of text to the file.

1. Type **EDLIN B:SCREEN.TXT** to retrieve your orginal text file.

2. Press <CR>.

The screen will show the response for editing the old file.  Edlin has read the file Screen.txt back into memory and informs you that this file is an old file by displaying "End of input file".

    A>EDLIN B:SCREEN.TXT
    End of input file
    *
    _

3. Type **1L**

4. Press <CR>.

Figure 5-11 shows the screen response for the List command 1L.

```
    *1L
            1:*GOOD MORNING,
            2:
            3:B & C OFFICE HELP SCREEN,
            4:
            5:Place your wordprocessing program disk in drive A:,

    *_
```

FIGURE 5-11.  List Command

## GUIDED ACTIVITY:  INSERTING NEW LINES

If you will notice, line 1 has an asterisk at the beginning of the line.  It means that this line is the active line.  If you press a carriage return now, line 2 will appear on the screen and you will be able to add text to that line.  If you want to add text to the last line of your file, you enter the command #I.  This will give you the next line number after your last line to add text.  If you know the next line number for your text entry, you can type the line number, then "I".  In the following example that, would be 6I.

1. Type **#I**

2. Press <CR>.

The screen response for the #I command is:.

```
    *#I
            6:*
```

3. Type **Don't forget to close the disk drive door.**

4. Press <CR>.

5. Type **Place your data disk in drive B:.**

6. Press <CR>.

7. Press <CTRL C> to end your present operation.

8. Type **1L** to list the lines.

9. Press <CR>.

Figure 5-12 shows the screen response for the added lines.

```
*1L
        1: GOOD MORNING.
        2:
        3: B & C OFFICE HELP SCREEN.
        4:
        5: Place your Wordprocessing program disk in drive A:.
        6: Don't forget to close the disk drive door.
        7: Place your data disk in drive B:.
*_
```

FIGURE 5-12.  List Added Lines

You are now going to add a text line in the middle of your file.  When you do this at line 6, all lines of text will move forward and be renumbered.

10. Type **6I**

11. Press <CR>.

12. Type **Make sure you will use the correct program disk.**

13. Press <CR>.

14. Type **Backup your files when you are done.**

15. Press <CR>.

16. Press <CTRL C>.

Figure 5-13 shows the screen response for the Insert command used with a line number at line 6.

```
    *6I
              6:*Make sure you will use the correct program disk,
              7:*Backup your files when you are done,
              8:*^C
    *_
```

FIGURE 5-13.  Line Number Insertion

**GUIDED ACTIVITY:  EDIT COMMAND**

You should be at the Edlin asterisk prompt.

1. Type **6**

2. Press <CR>.

There are two methods of copying characters across a line.  The first method is to press the <right arrow> key.  As you do, the character on the existing line will be copied to the new line.  The other method is to press the <F2> key and a character at the point where you want to move.  For example, if you want to move to the character "w" in line 6, you would press <F2>, then "w", and the cursor would move to the first occurrence of a "w" in the line.

3. Press <RIGHT ARROW> until your cursor is under the letter w in the word "will".

4. Press <LEFT ARROW> until you reach the beginning of the line.

5. Press <F2>.

6. Type **w**

7. Type **use the correct program disk.**

8. Press <CR>.

9. Type **6**

10. Press <CR>.

11. Press <F2>.

12. Type **p**

13. Press <INS>.  Pressing the Insert key will allow you to insert text into the line.

14. Type **Wordprocessing**

15. Press <SPACE BAR> one time.

16. Press <F3>.  This will copy the remainder of the text in the line.

17. Press <CR>.

18. Type **1L**

19. Press <CR>.

Figure 5-14 shows the screen results of editing a file.

```
*1L
        1: GOOD MORNING.
        2:
        3: B & C OFFICE HELP SCREEN.
        4:
        5: Place your Wordprocessing program disk in drive A:.
        6:*Make sure you use the correct Wordprocessing program disk.
        7: Backup your files when you are done.
        8: Don't forget to close the disk drive door.
        9: Place your data disk in drive B:.


*_
```

FIGURE 5-14.  Edit Command.


**GUIDED ACTIVITY:  COPY COMMAND**

You are going to copy a line in your file to another location.

Type the beginning line number followed by a comma, the end line number followed by a comma, the number sign and the letter c, followed by a semicolon.  To copy line 1 to the end of the file you would enter 1,1,#C;.

1. Type **1,1,#C;** to copy GOOD MORNING in line 1 to line 10.

2. Press <CR>.

3. Type **1L**

4. Press <CR>.

Figure 5-15 will show the results of copying a single line with the Copy command.

```
        1L
                1: GOOD MORNING,
                2:
                3: B & C OFFICE HELP SCREEN,
                4:
                5: Place your Wordprocessing program disk in drive A:,
                6: Make sure you use the correct Wordprocessing program disk,
                7: Backup your files when you are done,
                8: Don't forget to close the disk drive door,
                9: Place your data disk in drive B:,
               10:*GOOD MORNING,

        *_
```

FIGURE 5-15.  Copy Command

5. Type **2,3,11C;** to copy lines 2 and 3 to the end of the file.

6. Press <CR>.

7. Press <CTRL C>.

8. Type **1L**

9. Press <CR>.

Figure 5-16 shows the screen results of the Copy command.

```
*1L

     1: GOOD MORNING.
     2:
     3: B & C OFFICE HELP SCREEN.
     4:
     5: Place your Wordprocessing program disk in drive A:.
     6: Make sure you use the correct Wordprocessing program disk.
     7: Backup your files when you are done.
     8: Don't forget to close the disk drive door.
     9: Place your data disk in drive B:.
    10: GOOD MORNING.
    11:
    12:*B & C OFFICE HELP SCREEN.
 *_
```

FIGURE 5-16.  Copy Command

## GUIDED ACTIVITY:  MOVE COMMAND

The Move command can be used to move lines of text within your file.  If you want to reverse line 8 with line 9 in your file, you would issue the command 8,8,10M;.  Do not leave any spaces in the command, and do not include the period when you issue the command.  The command will cause line 8 to move in front of line 10 and line 9 to drop into the place of line 8.

1. Type **8,8,10M;**

2. Press <CR>.

3. Press <CTRL C>.

4. Type **1L**

5. Press <CR>.

Figure 5-17 shows the screen response of moving line 8 with the Move command.

```
    *1L

            1: GOOD MORNING.
            2:
            3: B & C OFFICE HELP SCREEN.
            4:
            5: Place your Wordprocessing program disk in drive A:.
            6: Make sure you use the correct Wordprocessing program disk.
            7: Backup your files when you are done.
            8: Place your data disk in drive B:.
            9: Don't forget to close the disk drive door.
           10:*GOOD MORNING.
           11:
           12: B & C OFFICE HELP SCREEN.

    *_
```

FIGURE 5-17.  Move Command

6. Type **5,5,7M;**

7. Press <CR>.

8. Press <CTRL C>.

9. Type **7,7,10M;**

10. Press <CR>.

11. Press <CTRL C>.

12. Type **1L**

13. Press <CR>.

Figure 5-18 shows the line changes from using the Move command with your file.

```
    *1L

         1: GOOD MORNING.
         2:
         3: B & C OFFICE HELP SCREEN.
         4:
         5: Make sure you use the correct Wordprocessing program disk.
         6: Place your Wordprocessing program disk in drive A:.
         7: Place your data disk in drive B:.
         8: Don't forget to close the disk drive door.
         9: Backup your files when you are done.
        10:*GOOD MORNING.
        11:
        12: B & C OFFICE HELP SCREEN.


    *_
```

FIGURE 5-18.  Line Changes with Move Command

### GUIDED ACTIVITY:  SEARCH COMMAND

It is often helpful to be able to find words or text within a file. Edlin gives you this availability with the Search command. In this activity, you will find the word GOOD with the Search command. To find the word in your file, you list the first line-number 1 followed by a comma, then the last line-number 12, followed by S (which stands for search), and the word you want to find. It is important not to leave any spaces in the command. The command looks like this:  1,12SGOOD. Do not use the period in the command.

1. Type **1,12SGOOD**

2. Press <CR>.

The screen response to the Search command is:

    *1,12SGOOD

        1:GOOD MORNING.

    *
    _

**GUIDED ACTIVITY:  SEARCH COMMAND WITH ?**

In this activity, you will use the Search command with a "?".  Using a question mark in your string command causes Edlin to search the file and upon finding the word specified, to ask you if it is the word. If you say yes, the search ends.  If you say no, the search will continue until the whole file has been searched.

1. Type **1,12?SGOOD**

2. Press <CR>.

3. Type **N**

4. Type **N**

Figure 5-19 shows the screen response for the 1,12S?GOOD command.  In line 1, Edlin asks if the word found is OK.  If you say "N," it will proceed to the next occurrence of the word and ask you again.  When it has gone through the whole file from line 1 through line 12, it will stop.

```
*1,12S?GOOD

        1:*GOOD MORNING.
O.K.? N
        10:GOOD MORNING.
O.K.?N
Not found
*_
```

FIGURE 5-19.  Search Command

5. Type **1,12?SGOOD**

6. Type <CR>.

7. Type **Y**

The screen response for the Search command is:

```
*1,12?SGOOD

        1; GOOD MORNING.

O.K.? Y
*
_
```

## GUIDED ACTIVITY:  REPLACE COMMAND

You can use the Replace command to find "MORNING", and replace "MORNING" with the word "NIGHT".  The command structure for the Replace command is similar to the Search command.  You must give the beginning line number, a comma, then the end line number, followed by a question mark, an "R" for the Replace command, then the word you are looking for.  You must separate the words you are looking for and the word you want to replace with a "^Z".  The characters "^Z" mean depress the <CTRL> key while pressing the <Z> key, then release the keys.  The command looks like this: 1,12?RMORNING^ZNIGHT.  Remember not to include the period in the command.

1. Type **1,12?RMORNING.^ZNIGHT.**

2. Press <CR>.

3. Type **N**

4. Type **Y**

Figure 5-20 shows the screen response to the Replace command using the string 1,12?RMORNING^ZNIGHT.

```
*1,12?RMORNING^ZNIGHT
        1:*GOOD NIGHT.
O.K.? N
        10: GOOD NIGHT.
O.K.? Y
*_
```

FIGURE 5-20.  Replace Command

5. Type **1L**

Figure 5-21 shows the screen response for the Replace (1L) command.

```
*1L
            1: GOOD MORNING.
            2:
            3: B & C OFFICE HELP SCREEN.
            4:
            5: Make sure you use the correct Wordprocessing program disk.
            6: Place your Wordprocessing program disk in drive A:.
            7: Place your data disk in drive B:.
            8: Don't forget to close the disk drive door.
            9: Backup your files when you are done.
           10:*GOOD NIGHT.
           11:
           12: B & C OFFICE HELP SCREEN.

    *_
```

FIGURE 5-21.  1L Command

**GUIDED ACTIVITY:  CLEAN UP AND SAVE YOUR FILE**

1. Type **11,12D**

2. Press <CR>.

3. Type **11I**

4. Press <CR>.

5. Press <CTRL C>.

6. Type **E**

7. Press <CR>.

8. Type **CLS**

9. Press <CR>.

10. Type **TYPE B:SCREEN.TXT** to view your finished file.

11. Press <CR>.

## COMMAND REVIEW DICTIONARY

In this unit, you have read about several DOS commands. Most have optional parameters. We have tried to cover both the common and the rarely used forms of each command. The following forms of this unit's commands are the most frequently used and should be reviewed carefully.

EDLIN Newfile.txt          loads Edlin and creates a new file.

EDLIN Oldfile.txt          loads Edlin and allows you to edit an old file.

I                          insert a line into an Edlin file.

L                          list up to 23 lines in an Edlin file.

Q                          to abort an Edlin file.

CTRL C                     to stop editing lines.

## REVIEW QUESTIONS

1. How do you quit Edlin without saving the text file?

2. What will Edlin do if you do not use a ? in the Search and Replace command?

3. Do you have to save your Edlin file on the same disk with Edlin.com?

4. What procedure would you follow to print an Edlin file on a printer?

## DOCUMENTATION RESEARCH

1. Research IBM DISK OPERATING SYSTEM Version 3.1 manual for DOS commands and parameters not used in class.

# UNIT

# 6

# THE INVISIBLE DOS COMMANDS

**SUPPLIES NEEDED**

The supplies that you will need for completing this unit are:

1. PC-DOS 3.10 program disk;
2. formatted 5-1/4 inch double-sided, double-density system diskette.

**OBJECTIVES**

After completing this unit, you will be able to:

1. build a Batch file;
2. build a Autoexec.bat file;
3. create a Config.sys file.

**IMPORTANT COMMANDS**

1. Echo command;
2. Pause command;
3. Buffers command;
4. Files command.

## ASSIGNMENTS

Place a check in front of the assignments for this unit:

1. ____    Guided Activity:  Create an Autoexec.Bat File.
2. ____    Guided Activity:  Create a Config.Sys File.
3. ____    Answer the Review Questions.
4. ____    Documentation Research.

## THE INVISIBLE DOS COMMAND

If you find during your work that you are entering the same commands each time you start your computer, a batch file (sometimes referred to as a bat file) can make your computing easier and more efficient. Bat files are programs you create which can be executed from the keyboard or from within other batch files, i.e., from within an Autoexec.bat file when your computer system is booted. The commands in your bat files respond the same way as if you were entering them from the keyboard. Bat files save you time because you only have to list the commands in the file then the file, does the work for you.

In this unit, you will create two kinds of bat files; one is called Autoexec.bat and the other is referred to simply as a bat file. An Autoexec.bat file is a special bat file executed from your root directory when you boot up your computer. When DOS sees an Autoexec.bat file, it executes the commands it finds in the file. A bat file is created the same way as the Autoexec.bat file but does not use the name Autoexec in its name. This way, DOS does not execute the file when you start your computer. Bat files can be executed by typing the filename and pressing the carriage return.

Bat files can be created with a text editor or Copy con. In this unit, you will create the bat file with Copy con; if you make any errors or want to add commands, you will do these tasks with Edlin.

## GUIDED ACTIVITY:  STARTING THE COMPUTER

1. Insert the DOS 3.1 program diskette in drive A: and shut the drive door.

2. Turn on the computer.

3. Enter the current date and time.

4. Place a 5-1/4 formatted system diskette in drive B:.

## GUIDED ACTIVITY:  YOUR FIRST BAT FILE

To better understand bat files, let's make a small one. Remember, when using Copy con you can only make corrections to the line you are on. Once you press the <carriage return> you will not be able to return to that line to make corrections. If you make an error and want to cancel Copy con and start over press <CTRL C>, and the file will be cancelled.

1. Type **COPY CON B:HELLO.BAT**

2. Press <CR>.

The Echo Off command will stop commands used in your files from appearing on your screen when the file is executed, but you will see the results of the command.

3. Type **ECHO OFF**

4. Press <CR>.

The Cls command will clear your screen of all characters that are displayed up to the point you used the command.  Sometimes, it is helpful to remove the previous instructions or clutter from the screen in order to avoid confusion.

5. Type **CLS**

6. Press <CR>.

The Echo command will display the contents of a line to the screen.

7. Type **ECHO HELLO!**

8. Press <CR>.

9. Type **ECHO It sure is a good day to learn DOS!**

10. Press <CR>.

11. To end the file with press <CTRL Z> or press <F6>.

12. Press <CR>.  The HELLO.BAT file is now stored on drive B:.

13. Type **B:HELLO**

14. Press <CR>.

Your screen will respond with the following message:

    HELLO!
    It sure is a good day to learn DOS!


**GUIDED ACTIVITY:  ADDING INVISIBLE LINES TO THE HELLO.BAT FILE WITH EDLIN**

If you decide you need some space in your bat file, you can insert invisible lines with the Echo command. When you type "ECHO:" into the file, DOS will leave a blank line at that point.

1. Type **EDLIN B:HELLO.BAT**

2. Press <CR>.

3. Type **1L**

4. Press <CR>.

5. Type **4I**

6. Press <CR>.

7. Type **ECHO:**

8. Press <CR>.

9. Type **ECHO:**

10. Press <CR>.

11. Type **ECHO:**

12. Press <CR>.

13. Type **ECHO:**

14. Press <CR>.

15. Press <F6>.

16. Press <CR>.

17. Type **E**

18. Press <CR>.  The changed HELLO.BAT file is now saved to drive B:.

19. Type **B:HELLO**

20. Press <CR>.

The screen response shows that the Hello.bat file now has four blank lines between the "HELLO!" and "It sure is a good day to learn DOS".

HELLO!




It sure is a good day to learn DOS!

## GUIDED ACTIVITY:  TERMINATE A BATCH FILE

There will be times when you want to stop a bat file.  If you press <CTRL C>, DOS will stop the bat file and respond with the message "Terminate batch job (Y/N)?".  If you press "Y" the bat file will be cancelled and the DOS prompt will return.

1. Type **B:HELLO.BAT**

2. Press <CR>.

Because you have a small bat file, you will have to be fast with the CTRL C keystroke to stop the file.

3. Press <CTRL C>.

## GUIDED ACTIVITY:  STOPPING THE BAT FILE WITH PAUSE COMMAND

If the file executed too fast for you and you still want to stop it, use the Pause command in your file.  The Pause command will stop a bat file to allow you the time needed to accomplish your task. For example, you might need to switch disks from one drive to another; Pause provides the time you need to do so.

1. Type **EDLIN B:HELLO.BAT**

2. Press <CR>.

3. Type **1L**

4. Press <CR>.

5. Type **4**

6. Press <CR>.

7. Type **PAUSE**

8. Press <CR>.

9. Type **E**

10. Press <CR>.

11. Type **B:HELLO**

12. Press <CR>.

13. Press <CR> when you are ready to continue.

14. Type **B:HELLO**

15. Press <CR>.

16. Press <CTRL C>.

17. Type **Y**. You now have the following message on your screen:

> HELLO!
> Strike a key when ready...^C
>
> Terminate batch job (Y/N)? Y

## GUIDED ACTIVITY:  CREATING AN AUTOEXEC.BAT FILE

The Autoexec.bat file is a batch file placed in the root directory of your system.  Remember, when DOS starts your computer at bootup, it looks at the root directory and, if it finds a file named Autoexec.bat, it will execute the file and follow the commands within the file.  You are going to add the Date and Time commands, remove the Pause command, and place the Autoexec.bat file in the root directory of your disk.

1. Type **COPY CON B:AUTOEXEC.BAT**

2. Press <CR>.

3. Type **ECHO OFF**

4. Press <CR>.

5. Type **CLS**

6. Press <CR>.

7. Type **DATE**

8. Press <CR>.

9. Type **TIME**

10. Press <CR>.

11. Type **CLS**

12. Press <CR>.

13. Type **ECHO HELLO!**

14. Press <CR>.

15. Type **ECHO:**

16. Press <CR>.

17. Type **ECHO:**

18. Press <CR>.

19. Type **ECHO:**

20. Press <CR>.

21. Type **ECHO:**

22. Press <CR>.

23. Type **ECHO It sure is a good day to learn DOS!**

24. Press <CR>.

25. Press <F6>.

26. Press <CR>.  The Autoexec.bat is now stored on the disk in drive B:.


**GUIDED ACTIVITY:  REBOOTING THE COMPUTER WITH AUTOEXEC.BAT**

1. Remove the System disk from drive B: that contains the Autoexec.bat file and insert it into drive A:.

2. Reboot your computer.

3. Enter the current date.

4. Press <CR>.

5. Enter the current time.

6. Press <CR>.

Your screen should greet you with the results of your Autoexec.Bat file.

## CONFIGURATION SYSTEM FILE

The Configuration System file, or Config.Sys as it is most commonly called, is a file DOS uses at startup to configure your computer system. The Config.Sys file can change your DOS system in certain ways. When you start your system DOS looks in the Root directory to see if you have a Config.Sys file; if it finds that file, it will carry out the commands in the file. The commands you can have in a Config.Sys file are: Break, Buffers, Country, Device, Fcbs, Files, Lastdrive, and Shell.

In this unit you are going to deal with the Buffer and File commands because these commands are the ones most often changed when setting up application programs. If you are interested in the remaining commands, refer to your Disk Operating System Manual for their explanation and use.

## BUFFERS COMMAND

The Buffers command allows you to tell DOS how many buffers you want. A buffer is block of 528 bytes of memory that DOS can use to store data so it won't have to write data to and read data from your disks. You can have from 1 to 99 buffers with DOS 3.X. The advantage of buffers is that they speed up your computer operation; a disadvantage is that they use up the memory you might need for programs. The amount of memory available in your computer and the requirements of your application programs will determine the number of buffers you will use. The minimum number of buffers is 1 and the maximum number is 99, with a default value set for 2 for a PC, and 3 for an PC AT.

## FILES COMMAND

The Files command provides you with the ability to tell DOS how many files DOS can use at one time. Some application programs will require more than others. The minimum number of eight files is set by the DOS default setting. DOS allows the maximum number of files to be 255.

## GUIDED ACTIVITY:  CREATING A CONFIG.SYS FILE WITH COPY CON

1. Type **COPY CON CONFIG.SYS**

2. Press <CR>.

3. Type **BUFFERS=3**

4. Press <CR>.

5. Type **Files=10**

6. Press <CR>.

7. Press <CTRL Z>.

8. Press <CR>.

9. Type **DIR A:** to view the new Config.Sys file on your disk in drive A:.

If you want to take advantage of the Config.Sys file, you must reboot your computer.  DOS looks for the Config.Sys file only at startup.

## REVIEW QUESTIONS

1. In what directory do you place an Autoexec.bat file?

2. How would you stop a batch file during execution?

3. What procedure would you follow to insert a blank line within a batch file?

4. How many bytes of memory do five buffers use?

## DOCUMENTATION RESEARCH

1. Research IBM DISK OPERATING SYSTEM Version 3.1 manual for DOS commands not used in class.

# UNIT

# 7

# THE HARD DISK MANAGEMENT COMMANDS

## SUPPLIES NEEDED

The supplies that you will need for completing this unit are:

1. PC-DOS 3.10 program disk;
2. 5-1/4 inch double-sided, double-density formatted system diskette.

## OBJECTIVES

After completing this unit, you will be able to:

1. use the Mkdir command to make a subdirectory on a disk;
2. use the Chdir command to change to subdirectory on a disk;
3. use the Rmdir command to remove a subdirectory from a disk;
4. use the Tree command to view the directories and files on a disk;
5. use the Path command to direct information to and from directories.

## IMPORTANT COMMANDS

The important commands introduced in this unit are:

1. Mkdir command;
2. Chdir command;
3. Rmdir command;

4. Tree command;
5. Path command.

## ASSIGNMENTS

Place a check in front of the assignments for this unit:

1. ____ Guided Activity:  Make a Subdirectory on a Diskette.
2. ____ Guided Activity:  Copy a File to a Subdirectory.
3. ____ Guided Activity:  Change from the Root Directory to a Subdirectory.
4. ____ Guided Activity:  Change the Path DOS takes with the Path Command.
5. ____ Guided Activity:  Remove a subdirectory from your diskette.
6. ____ Review Questions.
7. ____ Documentation Research.

## HARD DISK MANAGEMENT COMMANDS

Imagine what it would be like if you only had one directory on a disk in which to store your files and programs.  After a while the disk would be become very slow and confusing to use.  You would have a hard time trying to find those files and programs.  DOS has solved this problem by giving you the ability to create subdirectories.

The root directory is the beginning directory on every disk; it is identified by the backslash following the disk drive name.  Subdirectories are directories created below the root directory.  A directory can have files, labels, and subdirectories.  The root directory of the double-sided diskette can hold 112 entries, whereas the root directory of a hard disk can hold 512 entries.  Subdirectories are not restricted to the number of entries they can contain.

The hard disk management commands Mkdir (Make Directory), Chdir (Change Directory), Rmdir (Remove Directory), Tree, and Path give you the opportunity to effectively manage your directories and DOS system.

Special Note:  You may find a difference between the screens in this unit and the screens displayed on your computer monitor.  All formatted DOS system diskettes have at least two hidden files (IBMBIO.com and IBMDOS.com).  Sometimes you may may find a third hidden (vendor) file on you disk.  In the guided activities, we did not show the third hidden (vendor) file.  If the third file is present on your diskette, the screens will vary from those shown in the text.

## GUIDED ACTIVITY:  STARTING THE COMPUTER

1. Insert the DOS 3.1 program diskette in drive A: and shut the drive door.

2. Turn on the computer.

3. Enter the current date and time.

4. Remove your DOS diskette from drive A:.

5. Place a 5-1/4 formatted system disk in drive A:.

## MKDIR COMMAND

The Mkdir or Md (make directory) command gives you the option of creating subdirectories. All subdirectories start from the root directory and move downward. Imagine that you are standing on the top floor of a building (the root directory) all the floors below the top floor or root would be called subdirectories. You have only one root directory on a disk and the root directory can hold 512 entries , but the subdirectories under the root directory can have as many subdirectories as the amount of disk space will allow.

Subdirectories follow the same conventions as files. In the exercise, we are going to create subdirectories for word processing (Word), Spreadsheet (Spd), Data base (Data), Utility (Util), and DOS programs.

## GUIDED ACTIVITY:  MAKING SUBDIRECTORIES

1. Type **MKDIR\WORD**

2. Press <CR>.

3. Type **MKDIR\SPD**

4. Press <CR>.

5. Type **MKDIR\DATA**

6. Press <CR>.

7. Type **MKDIR\UTIL**

8. Press <CR>.

9. Type **DIR**

10. Press <CR>.

Figure 7-1 shows the results of the Mkdir command.  Notice that in the expression "Directory of A:\," the backslash is the name and identification of the root directory.  The subdirectories Word, Spd, Data, and Util have the extension **<DIR>** which tells you they are subdirectories.

```
A>DIR

Volume in drive A has no label
Directory of A:\

COMMAND  COM  23210    3-07-85  1:43p
WORD         <DIR>    11-03-86  1:38a
SPD          <DIR>    11-03-86  2:03a
DATA         <DIR>    11-03-86  2:03a
UTIL         <DIR>    11-03-86  2:03a
        5 Files(s) 295936 bytes free

A>_
```

FIGURE 7-1.  Making Subdirectories

## CHDIR COMMAND

The Chdir or Cd (change directory) command allows you to change from the root directory to the subdirectory you specify in the command.  To change from the root to the Util directory, you would type **CHDIR\UTIL** and press the <carriage return>.

1. Type **CHDIR\UTIL**

2. Press <CR>.

3. Type **DIR** to view the Util directory.

4. Press <CR>.

Figure 7-2 shows the screen contents of the "\UTIL" directory and the response for the Dir command. Notice that the directory is now called "A:\UTIL." The single dot and double dot within the directory tell you you're not in the root directory. The single dot refers to the current directory and the double dot refers to the directory that is directly above the current directory. In the example, it is the root directory which is directly above the current directory. If you typed **DIR ..** and pressed the < carriage return >, you would see the files in the root directory.

```
A>DIR


Volume in drive has no label
Directory of A:\UTIL


    .          <DIR>     11-03-86   1:38a
    ..         <DIR>     11-03-86   1:38a
        2 File(s)   295936 bytes free



A>_
```

FIGURE 7-2.  Util Directory

**GUIDED ACTIVITY:  MAKING ANOTHER SUBDIRECTORY**

Another concept you should understand when dealing with subdirectories is the concept of pathnames. When you work with a file or subdirectory you must tell DOS where it is located. A pathname is the way DOS uses to find its files and subdirectories.

In this activity you are going to add a subdirectory below the "\Util" subdirectory. This new directory will be called "DOS." The pathname for the DOS subdirectory file is "\UTIL\DOS". Whenever you refer to this subdirectory you must use the full Pathname of "\UTIL\DOS". If you wanted to view the files on this subdirectory, for example, you would type the command syntax **DIR\UTIL\DOS** to view the files.

1. Type **MKDIR\UTIL\DOS**

2. Press <CR>.

3. Type **DIR\UTIL\DOS**

4. Press <CR>.

Figure 7-3 shows the screen response to your command. Notice that the subdirectory is now called A:\UTIL\DOS.

```
A>DIR

Volume in drive A has no label
Directory of  A:\UTIL\DOS

   .          <DIR>       11-03-86   3:54a
   ..         <DIR>       11-03-86   3:54a
        2 File(s)     294912 bytes free

A>_
```

FIGURE 7-3.  UTIL\DOS SUBDIRECTORY

**GUIDED ACTIVITY:  COPYING A FILE TO A SUBDIRECTORY**

In this activity you are going to copy a file to the subdirectory "\UTIL\DOS". To use your DOS commands with the subdirectories, you must use the subdirectory's name with the commands. To copy the file Chkdsk.com from the DOS diskette to the "\UTIL\DOS" subdirectory, you would type the following command syntax:  **COPY B:CHKDSK.COM A:\UTIL\DOS.**

1. Place your DOS diskette in drive B:.

2. Type **COPY B:CHKDSK.COM A:\UTIL\DOS**

3. Press <CR>.

4. Type **DIR\UTIL\DOS** to view the subdirectory.

5. Press <CR>.

Figure 7-4 shows the screen response for copying the file Chkdsk.com to the subdirectory "\UTIL\DOS".

```
A>DIR\UTIL\DOS

Volume in drive A has no label
Directory of  A:\UTIL\DOS

.               <DIR>      11-03-86  1:38a
..              <DIR>      11-03-86  1:38a
CHKDSK COM  9435          3-07-85  1:43p
        3 Files(s) 284672 bytes free

A>_
```

FIGURE 7-4.  Copying File to A:\UTIL\DOS Subdirectory

## PATH COMMAND

The Path command is an internal DOS command that is available after you have loaded DOS into your computer.  The Path command is used by DOS to enable it to find commands, as well as certain files which do not reside in the current default drive and directory.  When you initate a command, DOS first looks at the current drive and directory for the file or command, if it does not find it, you receive the error message: "Bad command or filename." If you place the correct pathname before the command or file, DOS will use that path to find and execute the command.  DOS will execute a file or command with the extensions of Com, Exe, or Bat.  For example, in your directory A:\UTIL\DOS you have the file Chkdsk.com.  If you want to execute the Chkdsk.com file from the root directory, you must use the command syntax "\UTIL\DOS\CHKDSK" because the file does not reside in the root directory.  This command syntax tells DOS to go to the directory "\UTIL\DOS" and execute the Chkdsk command.  Do not place the quotes in the commands.

A better way to use the Path command is to place the command in your Autoexec.bat file.  If you place the path command in the Autoexec.bat file it will be loaded into DOS every time you start your system. That way you can execute commands from any subdirectory listed by the Path command. Use the following command syntax to direct DOS to search every subdirectory, and search the A: and B: drive.

PATH=A:\;A:\WORD;A:\SPD;A:\DATA;A:\UTIL;A:\UTIL\DOS;B:\;

Don't forget the DOS Path command will only execute files with the Exe, Com, and Bat extension.

**GUIDED ACTIVITY:  NAMING THE PATH**

1. Type **CHKDSK**

2. Press <CR>.

The screen response for the command will be a "Bad command or filename," because DOS cannot find the Chkdsk.com file in the current directory.

    A>CHKDSK
    Bad command or filename


    A>_

3. Type **\UTIL\DOS\CHKDSK**

4. Press <CR>.

Figure 7-5 shows the screen response for the Chkdsk command.  This time the command was executed by DOS because a Path to the command was available to DOS.

```
A>\UTIL\DOS\CHKDSK

    362496 bytes total disk space
     38912 bytes in 2 hidden files
      5120 bytes in 5 directories
     33792 bytes in 2 user files
    284672 bytes available on disk

    655360 bytes total memory
    618304 bytes free

A>_
```

FIGURE 7-5.  Command

**GUIDED ACTIVITY:  RESETTING THE PATH COMMAND TO DEFAULT**

1. Type **PATH;** to reset the path to the default.

2. Press <CR>.

3. Type **CHKDSK** to be sure you really don't have a path for DOS.

4. Press <CR>.

You will receive the following screen response:

        A>CHKDSK
        Bad command or filename


        A>_


**GUIDED ACTIVITY:  SETTING A NEW PATH COMMAND**

The Path command will allow DOS to search any subdirectory in its pathname.  In the following example, if DOS does not find the file Chkdsk.com in the root directory, it will search in the Util subdirectory and in the DOS subdirectory for the file.

1. Type **PATH=A:\UTIL\DOS;**

2. Press <CR>.

3. Type **CHKDSK**

4. Press <CR>.

Figure 7.6 shows the screen response for the command.

```
A>CHKDSK

     362496 bytes total disk space
      38912 bytes in 2 hidden files
       5120 bytes in 5 directories
      33792 bytes in 2 user files
     284672 bytes available on disk

     655360 bytes total memory
     618304 bytes free

A>_
```

FIGURE 7-6.  Chkdsk Command

5. Type **PATH;** to reset the path back to the default.

6. Press <CR>.


**GUIDED ACTIVITY:  SETTING A PATH TO A DIFFERENT DRIVE**

In this activity DOS will be directed to find a file in another disk drive.  DOS will first check the current root directory then drive B:.

1. Type **PATH=B:\;**

2. Press <CR>.

3. Type **CHKDSK**

4. Press <CR>.

Figure 7-7 shows the screen response for the command.

```
A>CHKDSK

      362496 bytes total disk space
       38912 bytes in 2 hidden files
        5120 bytes in 5 directories
       33792 bytes in 2 user files
      284672 bytes available on disk

      655360 bytes total memory
      618304 bytes free

A>_
```

FIGURE 7-7.  Chkdsk Command


**TREE COMMAND**

The Tree command will give you the opportunity to see the whole structure of the directories on your disks.  If you use the "/F" parameter, you can also see the files in the subdirectories.

Since you changed the pathname to drive B:, DOS will check that drive for the Tree.com file.

1. Type **TREE/F**

2. Press <CR>.

3. DOS will scroll through the directories and list them for you.


**RMDIR COMMAND**

A time will come when you need to remove a subdirectory from your disk.  The Rmdir command will accomplish the task of removing the subdirectory, but not the files within the subdirectory.  Before you can remove a subdirectory from your disk, you first must remove all the files from that subdirectory; except the dot files within the subdirectory.  When you are ready to use the Rmdir command, you must use it from the directory above the one to be removed.  You may not remove the current or root directory.

1. Type **CD\** to return to the root directory.

2. Press <CR>.

3. Type **DIR** to be sure you are in the root directory.

4. Press <CR>.

Figure 7-8 shows the contents of the root directory.

```
A>DIR

Volume in drive A has no label
Directory of A:\

COMMAND  COM   23210  3-07-85  1:43p
WORD           <DIR>  11-03-86  1:38a
SPD            <DIR>  11 03-86  2:03a
DATA           <DIR>  11-03-86  2:03a
UTIL           <DIR>  11-03-86  2:03a
        5 Files(s) 284672 bytes free

A>_
```

FIGURE 7-8.  Root Directory

5. Type **DEL A:\UTIL\DOS\CHKDSK.COM** to delete the Chkdsk.com file from the"\UTIL\DOS" subdirectory.

6. Press <CR>.

7. Type **DIR\UTIL\DOS**.

8. Press <CR>.

Figure 7-9 shows that the file Chkdsk.com has been deleted from the subdirectory and all that remains are the Dot files.

```
A>DIR\UTIL\DOS

Volume in drive A has no label
Directory of  A:\UTIL\DOS

.            <DIR>      11-03-86  1:38a
..           <DIR>      11-03-86  1:38a
       2  Files(s) 294912 bytes free

A>_
```

FIGURE 7-9.  Deleted Chkdsk.Com Directory

 9. Type **RMDIR\UTIL\DOS**

10. Press <CR>.

11. Type **DIR\UTIL**

12. Press <CR>.

Figure 7-10 shows that the "\DOS" subdirectory has been removed from the "\UTIL" subdirectory.

```
A>DIR\UTIL

Volume in drive A has no label
Directory of   A:\UTIL

        .          <DIR>      11-03-86   1:38a
        ..         <DIR>      11-03-86   1:38a
        2   Files(s) 295936 bytes free

A>_
```

FIGURE 7-10.  Root Directory

## COMMAND REVIEW DICTIONARY

In this unit, you have read about several DOS commands.  Most have optional parameters. We have tried to cover both the common and the rarely used forms of each command.  The following forms of this unit's commands are the most frequently used and should be reviewed carefully.

| | |
|---|---|
| MKDIR\DOS | makes a subdirectory called DOS. |
| CHDIR\DOS | changes from the root directory to the subdirectory. |
| RMDIR\DOS | removes the subdirectory. |
| PATH=C:\DOS; | directs DOS to look in both the root directory and DOS subdirectory for commands. |
| TREE/F | allows you to see the directories and files on your disks. |

## REVIEW QUESTIONS

1. How would you execute an internal DOS command on a subdirectory in a different drive?

2. Where would you place the Path command so you would be able to initiate commands from a directory that you are not currently using?

## DOCUMENTATION RESEARCH

1. Research IBM DISK OPERATING SYSTEM Version 3.1 manual for DOS commands and parameters not used in class.

# APPLICATION

# B

## PART 1:  BUILDING A SUBDIRECTORY WITH THE MKDIR COMMAND

In the previous unit we discussed the use of the MKDIR command.  In this application, you will build a subdirectory on a 5 1/4 inch floppy system disk for your DOS files.

A. Create a subdirectory called DOS.

B. Create a subdirectory called DATA.

C. Copy all your DOS files to the DOS subdirectory.


## PART 2:  BUILD AN AUTOEXEC.BAT FILE WITH EDLIN

In this application, you will create an Autoexec.bat file on a floppy system disk.

A. Create an Autoexec.bat file and use the Path command to allow you to access DOS external commands from any directory or subdirectory.

B. Make a duplicate of the floppy disk with the Diskcopy command.

C. Turn the duplicate disk in to your instructor.

# UNIT

# 8

# THE ESOTERIC
# DOS COMMANDS

**SUPPLIES NEEDED**

The supplies that you will need for completing this unit are:

1. IBM DISK OPERATING SYSTEM version 3.1 manual;
2. PC-DOS 3.1 diskette;
3. data disk used in previous exercises;
4. a blank unformatted disk.

**OBJECTIVES**

After completing this unit, you will be able to

1. list and define standard PC-DOS devices;
2. list and define the default DOS standard devices;
3. explain the difference between a serial port and a parallel port;
4. explain one use of the Nul: device;
5. define DOS redirection and give an example using DOS commands;
6. redirect output to a new disk file;
7. append output to an existing disk file by using redirection;
8. explain the difference between pipes and filters;
9. list and use the DOS filters;
10. explain the parameters which may be used with the Sort filter;
11. explain the parameters which may be used with the Find filter;

12. discuss the ASCII collating sequence and how it affects the Sort filter;

## IMPORTANT COMMANDS

The important commands introduced in this unit are

1. Find command;
2. More command;
3. Sort command;

## ASSIGNMENTS

Place a check in front of the assignments for this unit.

1.____ Review and understand the following terms listed in the Computer Terms Dictionary (Appendix A): asynchronous port, parallel port, secondary storage, serial port and standard devices.
2.____ Guided Activity: Redirecting DOS Input and Output.
3.____ Guided Activity: The Sort and More Filters.
4.____ Guided Activity: The Find Filter.
5.____ Review Questions.
6.____ Documentation Research.

## STANDARD PC-DOS DEVICES

Despite covering a great deal of territory relative to DOS commands, we have yet to explore the area of **standard devices**. PC-DOS permits us that luxury because it assumes that all activities use the two default devices, one input and the other output--until we instruct the machine otherwise.

The default device for normal input operations is referred to as the console, specifically the console keyboard. The default output device is also the console, specifically the monitor screen. Thus the operating system looks to the console for input and output unless specified otherwise. As already implied, the keyboard and the display monitor compose the console. In DOS shorthand, the form of the parameter is simply "Con:". This parameter should look familiar because we used it in the Copy Con: command exercise.

As we consider additional standard devices, we must return to the basics of computing. What are standard input devices? What are standard output devices? The answer would include, in addition to the console, such items as a printer, modem, light pen, disk drives, etc. DOS is less concerned with the specific peripheral than it is with the method of interface. The standard devices are defined as **serial ports** or **parallel ports** rather than as modems or printers.

In the simplest terms, a serial port has the capability of transferring data one bit at a time. A serial port is often referred to as an **asynchronous port**. Asynchronous is the opposite of the synchronized transferral of data which is required of a parallel port. A parallel port transfers data at the rate of eight bits at a time (i.e., one byte at a time). Keep in mind that one byte equals one character;such as a number, letter, or special character. The transferral of eight bits must be handled concurrently so the eight bits represent the same character on the receiving end as they did on the transmitting end.

For the sake of clarity, the following table indicates which type of port the listed peripherals use:

| Device | Port |
| --- | --- |
| Light pen | Serial |
| Modem | Serial |
| Printer | Serial or parallel |
| Network printer | Serial |
| Tape backup unit | Serial |

The IBM PC family of computers is structured to include up to two serial ports and three parallel ports, so DOS establishes standard device names for that number of ports.

The following list includes the DOS reserved words for each standard device. These terms may not be used as filenames. They are "reserved" for specific functions, i.e., to refer to the devices indicated.

| Keyboard | Con: |
| --- | --- |
| Monitor screen | Con: |
| Null device | Nul: |
| Parallel port #1 | Lpt1: |
| Parallel port #2 | Lpt2: |
| Parallel port #3 | Lpt3: |
| Serial port #1 | Com1: |
| Serial port #2 | Com2: |

Two of the above standard devices have aliases. The following two standard devices may be referred to using the listed reserved words:

| Parallel port #1 | Prn: |
| --- | --- |
| Serial port #1 | Aux: |

It may be easier to remember the reserved words used to identify these standard devices if you know the root words from which they are derived.

| Aux: | Auxiliary device |
| --- | --- |
| Com: | Communications port |
| Con: | Console |
| Lpt: | Line printer |
| Prn: | Printer |

Even though we have referred to each device name as ending with a colon, the colon is optional. For example, the line printer #1 may be called Prn or Prn: or Lpt1: or Lpt1.

Each of the reserved words representing a device may be used to substitute for a filename in a DOS command. We'll explore several examples in which this is the case.

A note on the Nul: standard device may be helpful. It is useful as a programmer's tool and can be used to substitute temporarily for an input or output device in the early stages of creating software. Further, Nul: can assist in the diagnosis of hardware and software problems. When a problem is encountered, the first step is to determine if the error is hardware- or software-related. By substituting Nul: for the input or output device stipulated in the software, a determination can be made on where the "bug" or problem is located. After substituting Nul:, if the program runs with the same errors, the problem is most likely software-related. If the program runs without errors after the Nul: substitution, the problem is with the input or output device which was replaced by Nul:.

## REDIRECTION OF STANDARD INPUT AND OUTPUT

The ability to redirect standard input and output is built into DOS. It enables a program to accept input from a device or file other than the standard default device or file. The same principle applies to output. Earlier, we indicated that the console (Con:) is the default I/O device for DOS. If the default devices were always used, then all input for any program would be restricted to the keyboard. Further, only the monitor screen could receive output. Such a situation would limit the value of the computer because output could not be directed to modems or printers. Further, input could not be accepted from light pens, modems, graphic tablets, or any other peripheral. Redirection of standard input and output devices eliminates this restriction.

A specific example might help. The Dir command lists to the screen a directory of all files on a specified diskette. For example, assume that the disk is in drive A: and holds the following files:

    FORMLTR.DOC
    HMBUDGET.WS
    ADDRESS.DBF
    ADDRESS.NDX
    ADDRESS.DBS
    FORMLTR.BDC
    HMBUDGET.BWS

If the command "Dir A:" is entered via the keyboard, where does the standard input for the command come from? Where does the standard output go? The input for the command obviously comes from the disk in the A: drive. Dir reads the directory table and displays the output, i.e., the list of files, to the console. In a literal sense, the command is

    DIR A: CON:

where A: indicates the standard input and Con: indicates the standard output. This syntax is inaccurate; it is shown only to explain that the output device is "understood" to be the console (specifically, the monitor screen).

Suppose it was important to obtain a complete listing of all files on a disk in printed form. With a short listing, like the example above, the PRTSC (print screen) key can be used. Suppose the disk included 70-80 different files. The solution is to redirect input from the Dir command to the printer. The symbol for DOS redirection is the greater-than or less-than sign ( < or > ).

To redirect the output from the Dir command to the printer, we would enter the following command:

    DIR A:>PRN

Remember that Prn is an alias for Lpt1:, so it is assumed that a printer is attached to parallel port #1. With the exception of Nul:, it is important to always have a device (printer, modem, etc.) attached to the standard device indicated.  If output is redirected to a nonexistent device, the computer will freeze--at best.  The results can be even more unpredictable.

Notice that the greater-than or less-than signs used to stipulate redirection serve as pointers indicating the flow of data.  Consider them the head of an arrow.  In the above example, the directory listing is redirected from the A:  drive input to Prn; i.e., the parallel printer.

If the objective was to create a file in which the directory data was stored, a slightly different version of the Dir command could be used.

    DIR A:>B:FILELIST.DOC

This command would create a new file on the diskette in drive B:  which would store all the directory data for files on the disk in the A:  drive.  In both of the examples used to date, the console screen would not display the directory listing.  In each example, the output has been redirected away from the monitor screen to another device (Prn) or to a file (FILELIST.DOC).

In the example which created the FILELIST.DOC file, we actually wish to add several additional files on a second diskette to the file named FILELIST.DOC.  To understand how to accomplish the appending of new data to an old file, we must first understand how output redirection works.  If a file is to be created via redirection, DOS first determines if a file with the same filename already exists on the target drive.  If it does not exist, DOS creates the file.  However, if the file already exists, DOS sets the write pointer to the beginning of the existing file.  In effect, the old file is overwritten by the redirected data.

If we switched the disk in drive A:  and entered the command

    DIR A:>B:FILELIST.DOC

then the directory data for files on the new disk would be written to the file FILELIST.DOC.  The previous data would be overwritten.

By using a double > > or double < <, the redirected data is appended to the file rather than overwriting it.  The important point to remember is that simple redirection to a file (using > or < ) will destroy an old file with the same filename.  However, the append redirection symbol (using > > or < < ) will add the new data to the end of the old file.

**GUIDED ACTIVITY:  REDIRECTING DOS INPUT AND OUTPUT**

In this Guided Activity you will use the DOS redirection capability to redirect first output, then input.

1. If your DOS diskette is write-protected, remove the write protection tab, for this exercise only.

2. Insert DOS diskette in drive A: and boot system.

3. Enter date and time when prompted.

4. Type **DIR > FILELIST**

5. Press <CR>.

The previous step generates a directory listing but then redirects it to a file called FILELIST on the disk in the A: drive, i.e., your DOS diskette.

6. Type **DIR FILELIST**

7. Press <CR>.

Figure 8-1 displays the screen response.  Notice that a new file resides on your DOS diskette.  The date and time portion of the directory listing will correspond to the date and time maintained by your computer when the file was created.

```
Volume in drive A: has no label
Directory of A:\

FILELIST         1614        11-01-86        12:50p

    1 File(s)         59392 bytes free

A>_
```

FIGURE 8-1.  Dir Listing for FILELIST

8. Type **TYPE FILELIST**

9. Press <CR>.

Your screen will display the complete directory listing as created by the Dir command and stored earlier in FILELIST. The output redirected to FILELIST can now be redirected to the printer using the Type command and DOS redirection.

10. Be sure your printer is turned on and the paper is set to the top of the form.

11. Type **TYPE FILELIST > PRN**

12. Press <CR>.

The printed report should appear as shown in Figure 8-2.

```
        Volume in drive A has no label
        Directory of  A:\

        ANSI         SYS      1651     3-07-85     1:43p
        ASSIGN       COM      1509     3-07-85     1:43p
        ATTRIB       EXE     15091     3-07-85     1:43p
        BACKUP       COM      5577     3-07-85     1:43p
        BASIC        COM     17792     3-07-85     1:43p
        BASICA       COM     27520     3-07-85     1:43p
        CHKDSK       COM      9435     3-07-85     1:43p
        COMMAND      COM     23210     3-07-85     1:43p
        COMP         COM      3664     3-07-85     1:43p
        DISKCOMP     COM      4073     3-07-85     1:43p
        DISKCOPY     COM      4329     3-07-85     1:43p
        EDLIN        COM      7261     3-07-85     1:43p
        FDISK        COM      8173     3-07-85     1:43p
        FIND         EXE      6403     3-07-85     1:43p
        FORMAT       COM      9398     3-07-85     1:43p
        GRAFTABL     COM      1169     3-07-85     1:43p
        GRAPHICS     COM      3111     3-07-85     1:43p
        JOIN         EXE     15971     3-07-85     1:43p
        KEYBFR       COM      2289     3-07-85     1:43p
        KEYBGR       COM      2234     3-07-85     1:43p
        KEYBIT       COM      2177     3-07-85     1:43p
        KEYBSP       COM      2267     3-07-85     1:43p
        KEYBUK       COM      2164     3-07-85     1:43p
        LABEL        COM      1826     3-07-85     1:43p
        MODE         COM      5295     3-07-85     1:43p
        MORE         COM       282     3-07-85     1:43p
        PRINT        COM      8291     3-07-85     1:43p
        RECOVER      COM      4050     3-07-85     1:43p
        RESTORE      COM      5410     3-07-85     1:43p
        SELECT       COM      2084     3-07-85     1:43p
        SHARE        EXE      8304     3-07-85     1:43p
        SORT         EXE      1664     3-07-85     1:43p
        SUBST        EXE     16611     3-07-85     1:43p
        SYS          COM      3727     3-07-85     1:43p
        TREE         COM      2831     3-07-85     1:43p
        VDISK        SYS      3307     3-07-85     1:43p
        FILELIST                 0    11-01-86    12:50p
            37 File(s)          59392 bytes free
```

FIGURE 8-2.  Report Generated by Redirection of FILELIST

For the record, FILELIST was created by the redirection of input from the default standard device, i.e. console, to a file created to store the directory listing. At the point when DOS created FILELIST, it was an empty file...in other words 0 bytes long. The DOS Dir command thus listed it with a 0 byte size and redirected that listing to the file itself. After the redirection is complete, the file is closed and DOS records (in the disk directory) the true size of the newly created file.

The length of the file was not determined until after the directory listing was completed--thus the data on FILELIST says the file is 0 bytes long. Subsequently the Dir command, see Figure 8-1, indicates that FILELIST consumes 1614 bytes of disk space.

In the remainder of this Guided Activity you will create a file which through redirection will provide input for a DOS command. Remember that when using the Format command, three keystrokes are required from the keyboard. After invoking the command Format B:, the user is instructed to insert a disk in the designated drive and press the ENTER key (first keystroke). After formatting is complete, the user is asked if another disk should be formatted. The response is either Y for yes or N for no (second keystroke), followed by pressing the ENTER Key (third keystroke).

You will use Edlin to create a text file containing these three keystrokes called INPUTS. Then INPUTS will be used through redirection to supply the keystrokes expected by DOS when it executes the Format command.

13. Type **EDLIN INPUTS**

14. Press <CR>.

The screen should respond with the Edlin prompt:

    New file
    *
    _

15. Press <I>.

16. Press <CR>.

17. Press <CR> again. This is the first keystroke expected by the Format command.

18. Press <N>. This is the second keystroke.

19. Press <CR>.

20. Press <CR>. This is the third keystroke.

21. Press <^C>.

22. Press <L>.

23. Press <CR> to display this short INPUTS file.

The screen should appear as shown in Figure 8-3.

```
A>EDLIN INPUTS
New file
*I
        1:*
        2:*N
        3:*
        4:*^C

*L
        1:
        2: N
        3:

*_
```

FIGURE 8-3.  Screen Display While Creating INPUTS File

24. Press <E>.

25. Press <CR> to exit and save the INPUTS file.

26. Insert a blank unformatted disk in drive B:.

27. Type **FORMAT B: < INPUTS**

Double-check the above line.  If you have not typed the command correctly, use the <BACK SPACE> key to erase incorrect characters, and retype the line before proceeding!

Once you press the ENTER key, this command is off and running.  By redirecting input from the INPUTS file, you lose control after pressing the ENTER key.

28. Press <CR>.

Figure 8-4 shows the screen response. By the time the DOS prompt returns, the disk in drive B: is formatted.

```
A>FORMAT B: <INPUTS
Insert new diskette for drive B:
and strike ENTER when ready

Formatting...Format complete

      362496 bytes total disk space
      362496 bytes available on disk

Format another (Y/N)?N
A>
```

FIGURE 8-4.  Screen Display of Format Command Using Redirection from INPUTS File

29. Type **COPY INPUTS B:** and Press <CR>. You will use this file again for a later exercise.

## PIPES AND FILTERS: DOS BUILDING BLOCKS

In home construction, pipes are used to convey material (gas, air, water) from one location to another. Filters, on the other hand, are used to alter material passing through the home. A furnace filter eliminates dust from the forced-air system; thus it alters the material (air) being piped throughout the house.

DOS pipes and filters function in parallel ways. Piping allows the output from one program or command to be used as the input for another program or command. In a sense it directs the standard output to become the input for another operation. The programs or commands become chained together. A pipe is indicated using the | character. For clarification, there is a difference between piping and redirection. Piping can serve as a connection between DOS commands, i.e., output from the first command becomes the input for the second command. It can also connect programs or subroutines. Redirection only deals with devices. The output of data may be redirected to the printer, a modem, or the console. You cannot redirect data to another DOS command.

The DOS piping operation creates one or more temporary files in the root directory of the default drive. DOS 2.0 names these files %PIPEx.$$$, where x is an integer. DOS versions 3.0 and higher create files using an eight-digit hexadecimal number based on output from the IBM PC's internal clock. It is important that these files not be erased until the piping operation is complete.

DOS filters accept data from standard input sources and then modify the data. The are three standard DOS filters are Sort, More, and Find.

## THE SORT FILTER

The most commonly used and easily understood filter is Sort. Sort is an external DOS command that manipulates text data which it receives as input and then outputs the data in sorted form. With DOS 2.0 and earlier, the sort is performed using the ASCII collating sequence. Beginning with DOS 3.1, a modified ASCII collating sequence is used.

In the ASCII collating sequence, each alphabetical and numerical character is assigned a binary value. There are significant differences between the ASCII text sort and a regular alphabetic or numeric sort. The left column below lists selected characters in random order, while the right column lists the same characters after an ASCII text sort such as would be generated by DOS 2.1 or earlier.

| | |
|---|---|
| junk5mail | # |
| 20 | % |
| z | 1 |
| Apple | 10 |
| 710 | 101 |
| APPLE | 20 |
| Zoo | 710 |
| 10 | 99 |
| junkmail | APPLE |
| 1 | Apple |
| junk mail | Zoo |
| 101 | apple |
| 99 | junk mail |
| % | junk5mail |
| apple | junkmail |
| # | z |

By examining the above example, it should become obvious that the ASCII text sort more closely approximates an alphabetic rather than numeric sort. However, the results are still puzzling until you recognize that uppercase alphabetic characters are considered completely different characters from lowercase characters. Thus the letter "a" follows the letter "Z" in this type of sort. Characters are evaluated beginning with the leftmost character. Numbers are not necessarily put in numeric order. Remember, each character place is assigned an ASCII value and then sorted based on that value. The range of values is outlined in the following table:

character(s)
(in ASCII collating sequence)


space (considered as a character)
special characters ( @, #, $, %, ^, &, etc.)
numbers (in ascending order: 0, 1, 2, 3, 4, 5, 6, 7, 8, 9)
uppercase letters ( A, B, C, D, E, F, G, H, etc.)
lowercase letters ( a, b, c, d, e, f, g, h, etc.)

Each special character and each non-printing character (<SHIFT> key, <CTRL> key, <ALT> key) is assigned an ASCII value If the ASCII text sort is not understood, then the DOS 2.1 Sort filter will generate some unexpected results.

Effective with DOS 3.1, a modification was made to the sort based on binary values.  The ASCII collating sequence is still used, with one exception.  Lowercase letters, a-z, are given equal value to uppercase letters, A-Z.  The following table demonstrates the effect of the different sorts:

| Random Elements | DOS 2.1 Sort | DOS 3.1 Sort |
|-----------------|--------------|--------------|
| APPLE | APPL | APPL |
| APPL | APPLE | APPLE |
| apple | LIME | apple |
| orange | apple | LIME |
| LIME | orange | orange |

For the duration of our discussion of the Sort filter, we'll assume use of DOS 3.1 or higher.

In a previous example, we wrote directory information from a disk directly to the printer.  That command form was

DIR A:>PRN

For the next few examples, we'll expand the file listing from an earlier example to include the following directory listing:

| FORMLTR | DOC | 14496 | 10-22-86 | 8:12p |
| HMBUDGET | WS | 11717 | 9-14-85 | 12:47a |
| ADDRESS | DBF | 98373 | 8-15-86 | 10:30p |
| ADDRESS | NDX | 963 | 8-15-86 | 10:30p |
| ADDRESS | DBS | 1123 | 8-15-86 | 10:30p |
| FORMLTR | BDC | 13888 | 10-09-86 | 7:22p |
| HMBUDGET | BWS | 9124 | 8-13-85 | 1:05p |

The command used to generate a random listing of files could be modified to print an ASCII text sorted directory.  Assuming that the A:  drive is the default drive, the command would be entered as

DIR|SORT>PRN

If the default drive were not A:, then the command would be entered as

DIR A:|SORT>PRN

Either command would generate a printed report like the following:

| ADDRESS | DBF | 98373 | 8-15-86 | 10:30p |
|---------|-----|-------|---------|--------|
| ADDRESS | DBS | 1123 | 8-15-86 | 10:30p |
| ADDRESS | NDX | 963 | 8-15-86 | 10:30p |
| FORMLTR | BDC | 13888 | 10-09-86 | 7:22p |
| FORMLTR | DOC | 14496 | 10-22-86 | 8:12p |
| HMBUDGET | BWS | 9124 | 8-13-85 | 1:05p |
| HMBUDGET | WS | 11717 | 9-14-85 | 12:47a |

**SORT PARAMETERS**

The Sort filter includes two optional parameters. The sort can be created in reverse ASCII text sort order, i.e., 9 is sorted before 1 and Z before A. The syntax of the command would be

SORT/R

The second Sort parameter stipulates the column on which the sort will begin. Without this parameter, DOS assumes the sort to begin in column 1. The syntax of the second parameter is

SORT/+n

where n represents an integer.

The directory listing generated by the Dir command lists bits of data beginning in specific columns. Beginning column numbers for each bit of data are listed in the following table:

| Data | Column Number |
|------|---------------|
| Filename | 1 |
| Extension | 10 |
| File size | 14 |
| Date created | 24 |
| Time created | 34 |

By knowing the beginning column locations, the output of the Dir command may be sorted by filename, extension, file size, date created, or time created. Though it may not be very helpful, a directory of files by creation date in reverse ASCII text sort order may be generated by using the command form

DIR A:|SORT/R/+24>PRN

A slightly more useful form would be to sort by file size using

DIR A:|SORT/+14>PRN

## THE MORE FILTER

In the earlier discussion of the Dir command, the P parameter was explained.  It generates a screenful of directory listings at a time and then pause until the user strikes another key.  The More filter behaves in a similar manner.  It breaks data from the standard input device into blocks of one screen page each.  After displaying a full page of output, the message "--More--" appears on the screen.  Pressing any key causes the next screenful of data to be displayed.  The process will continue until all subsequent pages of data have been displayed.

The Type command is often used to glance at the contents of an ASCII text file.  A common problem in using the Type command is that the text scrolls off the screen before it can be read.  A practical solution is to use the Type command in combination with the More filter.  The following command form would display one screenful of the text file, LETTER.TXT, at a time:

TYPE A:LETTER.TXT|MORE

## GUIDED ACTIVITY:  THE SORT AND MORE FILTERS

In the last Guided Activity, you created a file called FILELIST.  Since DOS diskette files are typically stored in alphabetical order, this exercise will use the Sort filter coupled with the FILELIST file to list DOS external commands in reverse alphabetical order.

1. Type **TYPE FILELIST|SORT/R**

2. Press <CR>.

The screen will scroll the DOS filenames past in reverse order. When the scrolling ends, the bottom of your screen will list the files shown in Figure 8-5.

| | | |
|---|---|---|
| COMP | COM | 3664 |
| COMMAND | COM | 23210 |
| CHKDSK | COM | 9435 |
| BASICA | COM | 27520 |
| BASIC | COM | 17792 |
| BACKUP | COM | 5577 |
| ATTRIB | EXE | 15091 |
| ASSIGN | COM | 1509 |
| ANSI | SYS | 1651 |

FIGURE 8-5.  Screen Display Using Reverse Sort on FILELIST File

Note that we used the Type command rather than actually using a Dir command. Almost the same result could be generated by the next step. Do you understand the difference?

3. Type **DIR|SORT/R**

4. Press <CR>.

You should have seen two new files this time. They are temporary files created by the Sort command. The disk, for a brief period of time, had 40 files rather than 38. Remember, the DOS diskette has 36 files, FILELIST and INPUTS raise the total to 38, then the two temporary files are number 39 and 40.

5. Type **DIR**

This directory listing does not show the two temporary files. They are erased automatically after Sort is through using them.

In each of the preceding examples, the directory listing scrolls off the screen. The More filter can be used to generate one page of screen display at a time. The user must then press any key to proceed to the next page of screen display.

6. Type **DIR|SORT/R|MORE**

7. Press <CR>.

The screen display will appear as shown in Figure 8-6.

| | | | | |
|---|---|---|---|---|
| VDISK | SYS | 3307 | 3-07-85 | 1:43p |
| TREE | COM | 2831 | 3-07-85 | 1:43p |
| SYS | COM | 3727 | 3-07-85 | 1:43p |
| SUBST | EXE | 16611 | 3-07-85 | 1:43p |
| SORT | EXE | 1664 | 3-07-85 | 1:43p |
| SHARE | EXE | 8304 | 3-07-85 | 1:43p |
| SELECT | COM | 2084 | 3-07-85 | 1:43p |
| RESTORE | COM | 5410 | 3-07-85 | 1:43p |
| RECOVER | COM | 4050 | 3-07-85 | 1:43p |
| PRINT | COM | 8291 | 3-07-85 | 1:43p |
| MORE | COM | 282 | 3-07-85 | 1:43p |
| MODE | COM | 5295 | 3-07-85 | 1:43p |
| LABEL | COM | 1826 | 3-07-85 | 1:43p |
| KEYBUK | COM | 2164 | 3-07-85 | 1:43p |
| KEYBSP | COM | 2267 | 3-07-85 | 1:43p |
| BEYBIT | COM | 2177 | 3-07-85 | 1:43p |
| BEYBGR | COM | 2234 | 3-07-85 | 1:43p |
| KEYBFR | COM | 2289 | 3-07-85 | 1:43p |
| JOIN | EXE | 15971 | 3-07-85 | 1:43p |
| INPUTS | | 8 | 11-01-86 | 1:02p |
| GRAPHICS | COM | 3111 | 3-07-85 | 1:43p |
| GRAFTABL | COM | 1169 | 3-07-85 | 1:43p |
| FORMAT | COM | 9398 | 3-07-85 | 1:43p |
| FIND | EXE | 6403 | 3-07-85 | 1:43p |

--More--_

FIGURE 8-6.  First Screenful of Text Generated by Using More Filter

8. Press any key to see the second screenful of text.  The second screen will list in order the files shown in Figure 8-7.

| | | | | |
|---|---|---|---|---|
| FILELIST | | 1701 | 11-01-86 | 12:51p |
| FDISK | COM | 8173 | 3-07-85 | 1:43p |
| EDLIN | COM | 7261 | 3-07-85 | 1:43p |
| DISKCOPY | COM | 4329 | 3-07-85 | 1:43p |
| DISKCOMP | COM | 4073 | 3-07-85 | 1:43p |
| COMP | COM | 3664 | 3-07-85 | 1:43p |
| COMMAND | COM | 23210 | 3-07-85 | 1:43p |
| CHKDSK | COM | 9435 | 3-07-85 | 1:43p |
| BASICA | COM | 27520 | 3-07-85 | 1:43p |
| BASIC | COM | 17792 | 3-07-85 | 1:43p |
| BACKUP | COM | 5577 | 3-07-85 | 1:43p |
| ATTRIB | EXE | 15091 | 3-07-85 | 1:43p |
| ASSIGN | COM | 1509 | 3-07-85 | 1:43p |
| ANSI | SYS | 1651 | 3-07-85 | 1:43p |
| 99999999 | | 0 | | |
| 99999999 | | 0 | | |

Volume in drive A has no label
Directory of A:\

40 File(s)     56320 bytes free

FIGURE 8-7.  Second Screenful of Text Generated by More Filter

The last two files are the temporary ones created by the Sort command.  They will be given names by DOS based on the computer's internal clock.  The byte size will be zero, but the date and time will depend on when you actually executed the Sort command.

Finally, you will sort using the column parameter in the next two steps.  Column 14 is the beginning of the file size (in bytes) data from the directory.

9. Be sure your printer is turned on and the paper set to the top of the form.

10. Type **TYPE FILELIST|SORT/+14 > PRN**

11. Press <CR>.

The generated printer report will appear as shown in Figure 8-8.

12. Type **COPY FILELIST B:** and Press <CR>.  You will use this file again in a later exercise.

| FILELIST |  | 0 | 11-01-86 | 12:50p |
|----------|-----|-------|---------|-------|
| MORE | COM | 282 | 3-07-85 | 1:43p |
| GRAFTABL | COM | 1169 | 3-07-85 | 1:43p |
| ASSIGN | COM | 1509 | 3-07-85 | 1:43p |
| ANSI | SYS | 1651 | 3-07-85 | 1:43p |
| SORT | EXE | 1664 | 3-07-85 | 1:43p |
| LABEL | COM | 1826 | 3-07-85 | 1:43p |
| SELECT | COM | 2084 | 3-07-85 | 1:43p |
| KEYBUK | COM | 2164 | 3-07-85 | 1:43p |
| KEYBIT | COM | 2177 | 3-07-85 | 1:43p |
| KEYBGR | COM | 2234 | 3-07-85 | 1:43p |
| KEYBSP | COM | 2267 | 3-07-85 | 1:43p |
| KEYBFR | COM | 2289 | 3-07-85 | 1:43p |
| TREE | COM | 2831 | 3-07-85 | 1:43p |
| GRAPHICS | COM | 3111 | 3-07-85 | 1:43p |
| VDISK | SYS | 3307 | 3-07-85 | 1:43p |
| COMP | COM | 3664 | 3-07-85 | 1:43p |
| SYS | COM | 3727 | 3-07-85 | 1:43p |
| RECOVER | COM | 4050 | 3-07-85 | 1:43p |
| DISKCOMP | COM | 4073 | 3-07-85 | 1:43p |
| DISKCOPY | COM | 4329 | 3-07-85 | 1:43p |
| MODE | COM | 5295 | 3-07-85 | 1:43p |
| RESTORE | COM | 5410 | 3-07-85 | 1:43p |
| BACKUP | COM | 5577 | 3-07-85 | 1:43p |
| FIND | EXE | 6403 | 3-07-85 | 1:43p |
| EDLIN | COM | 7261 | 3-07-85 | 1:43p |
| FDISK | COM | 8173 | 3-07-85 | 1:43p |
| PRINT | COM | 8291 | 3-07-85 | 1:43p |
| SHARE | EXE | 8304 | 3-07-85 | 1:43p |
| FORMAT | COM | 9398 | 3-07-85 | 1:43p |
| CHKDSK | COM | 9435 | 3-07-85 | 1:43p |
| ATTRIB | EXE | 15091 | 3-07-85 | 1:43p |
| JOIN | EXE | 15971 | 3-07-85 | 1:43p |
| SUBST | EXE | 16611 | 3-07-85 | 1:43p |
| BASIC | COM | 17792 | 3-07-85 | 1:43p |
| COMMAND | COM | 23210 | 3-07-85 | 1:43p |
| BASICA | COM | 27520 | 3-07-85 | 1:43p |

```
    Directory of  A:\
       37 File(s)    59392 bytes free
    Volume in drive A has no label
```

FIGURE 8-8.  Report Generated by Sorting FILELIST Based on File Size

**THE FIND FILTER**

The third and final DOS filter is the Find command.  The Find filter seeks out occurrences of a specified text string in specified file(s).  This external DOS command follows the syntax

FIND textstring [d:][filename.ext]

If we sought to locate all occurrences of the phrase "Strategic Defense Initiative" in a file called EINSTEIN.DOC on the a: drive, then the command would be executed as

FIND "Strategic Defense Initiative" A:EINSTEIN.DOC

Without adding one of three possible parameters, the results would duplicate each line in which the text string appeared.  The results would appear as shown in figure 8-9.

----------

----------EINSTEIN.DOC
writing to you regarding a program called "Strategic Defense Initiative".
Yes, "Strategic Defense Initiative"  is the same as what has  affectionately
cannot support "Strategic Defense Initiative" as it is currently defined.

----------

FIGURE 8-9.  Results of Find Filter

It is important to note that the Find filter is case-sensitive.  The text string used as a parameter for the filter must be identical to the text sought.  In other words "Strategic Defense Initiative" will not match with "strategic defense initiative" or even "Strategic defense Initiative."  Further, the text string must be enclosed within quotation marks.

Multiple files may be searched using a single Find command.  If we sought all occurrences of "Strategic Defense Initiative" in files named EINSTEIN.DOC, STARWARS.TXT and SDI.DOC, the command would take the form of

FIND "Strategic Defense Initiative" A:EINSTEIN.DOC A:STARWARS.TXT A:SDI.DOC

The resulting screen display might appear as shown in figure 8-10, assuming that there were no occurrences of the test string in the SDI.DOC file.

```
----------EINSTEIN.DOC
writing to you regarding a program called "Strategic Defense Initiative."
Yes,  "Strategic Defense Initiative"  is the same as what has  affectionately
cannot support "Strategic Defense Initiative" as it is currently defined.
----------SDI.DOC
----------STARWARS.TXT
The technical title is "Strategic Defense Initiative."
More often the "Strategic Defense Initiative" is referred to as "STARWARS" by
```

FIGURE 8-10.  Results of Find Filter Search Through Multiple Files

Unfortunately, global filename characters such as the asterisk and question mark cannot be used in filenames or extensions used with the Find filter.  This is a severe limitation, specifically when you are searching through numerous files that might include the sought-after text string.

## THE FIND FILTER PARAMETERS

The Find command lists only the line of text on which the sought-after text string appears.  If no occurrences of the text string have been found, the display will list the filename but nothing else.  There may be times when knowing the relative line number would be helpful.  The N parameter lists the relative line number at the beginning of the line in which the sought-after text occurs.  When determining the relative line number, DOS begins counting at the first line in the file.  Blank lines are counted also. Figure 8.11 is an example of the listing created using the N parameter.

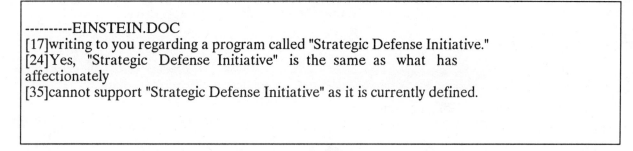

```
----------EINSTEIN.DOC
[17]writing to you regarding a program called "Strategic Defense Initiative."
[24]Yes, "Strategic  Defense  Initiative"  is  the  same  as  what  has
affectionately
[35]cannot support "Strategic Defense Initiative" as it is currently defined.
```

FIGURE 8-11.  Results of Search Using Find /N Parameter

Two additional parameters or switches may be used with the Find command. The basic Find command syntax searches through the named file(s) for lines of text which include the text string. This process can be reversed by using the /V parameter.

FIND/V "the" LETTER.TXT LETTER3.DOC

will list to the monitor screen all lines in the files LETTER.TXT and LETTER3.DOC which do not include the word "the".

The final parameter is the /C or "count" parameter. Rather than displaying the lines containing the text string, the /C parameter displays the number of lines which include the sought-after string. If we modified the command used to find occurrences of "Strategic Defense Initiative" to generate only a line count, the command would be

FIND/C "Strategic Defense Initiative" A:EINSTEIN.DOC A:STARWARS.TXT A:SDI.DOC

The screen display would list

----------EINSTEIN.DOC: 3
----------SDI.DOC: 0
----------STARWARS.TXT: 2

Whereas the /V and /N parameters may be combined, the count or C parameter cannot be combined with any other switch on a single occurrence of the Find command. If /C is used, the other switches are ignored.


## GUIDED ACTIVITY:  THE FIND FILTER

In this Guided Activity, you will create a text file using Edlin and then use the Find filter to locate occurrences of specific words within the file.

1. Be sure that your data diskette is in drive B: and that the DOS disk is in the A: drive.

2. Type **EDLIN B:FINDTEXT**

3. Press <CR>.

The screen will respond with the Edlin prompt:

New file
*
 _

4. Press <I>.

5. Press <CR>.

6. Type **This is a file in which to**

7. Press <CR>.

8. Type **test the Find Filter provided**

9. Press <CR>.

10. Type **by DOS 3.0 and higher.**

11. Press <CR>.

12. Press <CR> again.

13. Type **To test or not to test...**

14. Press <CR>.

15. Type **that is not the question.**

16. Press <CR>.

17. Type **Rather, the question is whether**

18. Press <CR>.

19. Type **Find can find the word test**

20. Press <CR>.

21. Type **or if the test will be failed.**

22. Press <CR>.

23. Press <CR> again.

24. Type **TEST PATTERN!**

25. Press <CR>.

26. Press <^C>.

Your screen should appear as shown in Figure 8-12.

```
A:>EDLIN FINDTEXT

New file
*I
     1:*This is a file in which to
     2:*test the Find Filter provided
     3:*by DOS 3.0 and higher.
     4:*
     5:*To test or not to test...
     6:*that is not the question.
     7:*Rather the question is whether
     8:*Find can find the word test
     9:*or if the test will be failed.
    10:*
    11:*TEST PATTERN!
    12:*^C

*_
```

FIGURE 8-12.  Edlin Test File Test

If the text in the file is not identical to that in Figure 8-12, use Edlin to go back and correct.

27. Press <E> to exit and save the file FINDTEXT.

28. Press <CR>.

29. Type **FIND "test" B:FINDTEXT**

30. Press <CR>.

The search conducted by the Find filter will display the messages shown in Figure 8-13.

```
---------- B:findtext
test the Find Filter provided
To test or not to test...
Find can find the word test
or if the test will be failed.
```

FIGURE 8-13.  Results of Find Search for "test"

31. Type **FIND "Test" B:FINDTEXT**

32. Press <CR>.

The Find filter is case-sensitive, so no occurrences of "Test" are found in the file.  The screen responds with

```
---------- B:findtext
```

meaning that the specified text was not found.

33. Type **FIND "TEST" B:FINDTEXT**

34. Press <CR>.

The screen response to this search appears in Figure 8-14.

```
---------- B:findtext
TEST PATTERN!
```

FIGURE 8-14.  Result of Find Search for "TEST"

35. Type **FIND/V "test" B:FINDTEXT**

36. Press <CR>.

The results of the search for lines without the text "test" are shown in Figure 8-15.

```
----------- B:findtext
This is a file in which to
by DOS 3.0 and higher.

that is not the question.
Rather, the question is whether

TEST PATTERN!
```

FIGURE 8-15.  Result of Find Search for Lines Without "test"

37. Type **FIND/C "test" B:FINDTEXT**

38. Press <CR>.

The monitor screen will display the results of the search as

```
---------- B:findtext: 4
```

There are four lines in the file FINDTEXT that include at least one occurrence of the specified text "test".

The final step will indicate the relative line numbers where the text "test" is found in the file.

39. Type **FIND/N "test" B:FINDTEXT**

40. Press <CR>.

The results of the command form are displayed in Figure 8-16.

```
----------- B:findtext
[2]test the Find Filter provided
[5]To test or not to test...
[8]Find can find the word test
[9]or if the test will be failed.
```

FIGURE 8-16.  Result of Find Search Using /N Parameter


## COMMAND REVIEW DICTIONARY

In this unit you have read about several DOS commands.  Most commands have optional parameters. We have tried to cover both the common and the rarely used forms of each command.  The following forms of this unit's commands are the most frequently used and should be reviewed carefully.

DIR A: >B:LIST.TXT — Creates an ASCII text file called LIST.TXT by redirection of the output from the Dir command.

DIR >PRN — Redirects the output from the Dir command to a printer connected to parallel port one.

DIR|MORE — Generates a listing of all files on the default drive, one screenful at a time.

DIR|SORT — Generates an alphabetical listing of all files on the default drive.

DIR|SORT/R — Generates a listing of all files on the default drive in reverse alphabetical order.

FIND "Germany" A:Country.doc — Locates all occurrences of the word **Germany** in the file Country.doc on the disk in drive A:.

FIND/N "Germany" A:Country.doc — Locates all occurrences of the word **Germany** in the file Country.doc on the disk in drive A: and indicates the relative line number on which each occurrence appears.

TYPE FILEONE.TXT >PRN — Redirects the listing created by the Type command to a printer connected to parallel port one.

## REVIEW QUESTIONS

1. Define the difference between a serial and parallel port.  Why is this a concern when discussing DOS standard devices?

2. How many DOS standard devices are there?  List them.

3. Which standard device(s) is/are considered the default device(s)?

4. Which standard device is typically used for debugging?  How would a programmer use this device?

5. If standard devices did not exist, other than the default device, how would computing be limited?

6. What does redirection of standard input and output mean?  Give an example.

7. When redirecting output to a disk file, how can the output be appended to an existing file?

8. Define DOS pipes and filters.  What is the difference?

9. What is the difference between a pipe and redirection?

10. What is the ASCII collating sequence?

11. What is the difference between the DOS 2.0 and 3.0 Sort filter?

12. In what order would the following filenames be sorted by DOS 2.0?  By DOS 3.0?

    Zebra
    cat
    Antelope
    939
    ANTELOPE
    CATwalk
    129
    93

13. What parameters are used with the Sort filter?

14. What parameters are used with the More filter?

15. What parameters are used with the Find filter?

## DOCUMENTATION RESEARCH

Read chapter 6 of the IBM DISK OPERATING SYSTEM version 3.1 manual which covers redirection, pipes, and standard I/O devices. Also read the pages from chapter 7 covering the More, Find, and Sort commands.

The DOS 1.x manual does not cover any of these commands or concepts. If using a DOS 2.x manual, refer to the pages in chapter 10 covering DOS filters, redirection of standard I/O devices, and piping to standard I/O devices. In the same chapter read the pages on the following commands: Find, More, and Sort.

1. When using the Find filter, will an uppercase text string match a lowercase text string in the search? This topic is not covered in the DOS 2.x manual.

2. Will the Find filter accept global wildcard characters in the filename to be searched?

3. Is it possible to search more than one file with a single Find command? If so, how?

4. What switches can be used with the More command?

5. What is the maximum file size that can be ordered with the Sort filter?

6. If the /+n parameter is not used with the Sort filter, what default value does n assume?

7. Can the input and output filename used with the Sort filter be identical? This topic is not covered in the DOS 2.x manual.

# APPLICATION

# C

**PART 1:  SEARCHING FOR TEXT PHRASES IN A FILE**

In the previous unit we discussed redirection and DOS filters.  In this application, you will search a text file for all occurrences of a specific phrase, and redirect the results to a printer.

A. Obtain a copy of the file "Search.txt" from your instructor.  This file is an ASCII text file.

B.  Use a DOS filter to find all occurrences of the phrase **He should have known better.**

C.  Redirect the results of the search to a printer.

D.  Repeat the above search for the phrase **He should have known better.**, however, this time you should redirect (to a printer) a listing of the relative line numbers where the phrase occurs in the file.

E.  Turn in a printed copy of the results to your instructor.

# UNIT

# 9

# MORE ESOTERIC DOS COMMANDS

**SUPPLIES NEEDED**

The supplies that you will need for completing this unit are:

1. IBM DISK OPERATING SYSTEM Version 3.1 manual;
2. PC-DOS 3.1 diskette;
3. data disks used in previous unit.

**OBJECTIVES**

After completing this unit, you will be able to

1. list the four uses of the Mode command;
2. explain the parameters associated with the communications protocol, including baud rate, parity, databits, and stopbits;
3. define a virtual drive;
4. rate the speed difference between a floppy disk drive, a fixed disk drive, and a virtual drive;
5. create a Print command queue;
6. define a print queue;
7. describe the benefits of a print queue;
8. list the most common parameters used with the Print command.

## IMPORTANT COMMANDS

The important commands introduced in this unit are

1. Mode command;
2. Print command;
3. Vdisk command.

## ASSIGNMENTS

Place a check in front of the assignments for this unit.

1.____ Review and understand the following terms listed in the Computer Terms Dictionary (Appendix A):  background task, baud, bit, byte, databits, foreground task, parity, print queue, protocol, stopbits, terminal program, time-out, virtual drive, and word size.
2.____ Guided Activity:  The Print Mode Option.
3.____ Guided Activity:  Using the Virtual Drive.
4.____ Guided Activity:  Creating a Print Queue.
5.____ Review Questions.
6.____ Documentation Research.

## FOUR MODES OF OPERATION

The Mode command is used to accomplish four seemingly unrelated functions, though each does in fact affect the mode of operation of the microcomputer system.  The Mode command has four options or formats:

1. setting the format of printer output;
2. switching monitor display mode;
3. setting protocol for a serial port;
4. redirecting parallel port output to a serial port.

## THE MODE COMMAND:  CHANGING PRINTER OUTPUT

Printer output can be affected by using the following Mode command syntax:

    MODE  LPTn[:][c][,l]

where n represents the printer port number (i.e., Lpt1, Lpt2 or Lpt3), c represents the characters per line and l is the lines per vertical inch.

The power-on default value for this Mode command option is

MODE  LPT1:80,6

The options are limited.  For vertical lines per inch, only two values may be used: 6 or 8.  Similarly, only the values 80 or 132 may be used for characters per inch.

## THE MODE COMMAND:  CHANGING DISPLAY ADAPTERS

The second Mode command option is to set the kind of display monitor adapter expected by the system and indicate the number of characters displayed vertically across the screen.  The syntax of this option is

MODE  [d][,s][,t]

where d represents the display adapter type and characters across the screen, s shifts the screen right or left, and t generates a test pattern.

The display adapter/width options are listed below.

BW40        Disables color after switching to the color/graphics display adapter and generates 40 characters per line across the screen in monochrome.

BW80        Disables color after switching to the color/graphics display adapter and generates 80 characters per line across the screen in monochrome.

40          Displays 40 characters per line on the color/graphics display adapter.

80          Disables 80 characters per line on the color/graphics display adapter.

CO40        Enables color after switching to the color/graphics display adapter and generates 40 characters per line across the screen.

CO80        Enables color after switching to the color/graphics display adapter and generates 80 characters per line across the screen.

MONO        Causes the monochrome display adapter to be the active display adapter and generates 80 characters per line across the screen.  There is no 40-character option with the monochrome display adapter.

This option of the Mode command may be used to shift the screen display slightly to the right or left.  To switch right, the R parameter is used.  L switches the display to the left.  The type of display adapter must be stipulated in the command.

If you are working with a monochrome display adapter and monitor, the form of these commands would be

    MODE  MONO,R
    MODE  MONO,L

In the 40-column mode, the R or L shifts the screen one character in the specified direction. In 80-column mode, the shift is two characters to the right or left, as indicated.

To generate a test pattern for a color/graphics display and shift the screen right, the following command form may be used:

    MODE  CO80,R,T

When combining the T parameter with a right or left shift, a screen message will ask if the monitor image is properly aligned. If you respond with no, the screen will shift again in the direction originally indicated. A yes response concludes the command and the test pattern disappears.

## THE MODE COMMAND:  SETTING SERIAL PROTOCOL

Earlier in this chapter the difference between an asynchronous port (serial) and a parallel port was discussed. One function of the mode command is to set or initialize the parameters used by the serial or asynchronous port. These parameters are often referred to as **protocol**. Computers which communicate using data communications or telecommunications must speak the same language. They must speak at the same rate, i.e., **baud** rate; speak in uniform **word sizes**, i.e., **databits**; and know when communication ends, i.e., **stopbits**. The two computers must also know how error checking occurs so that signals scrambled over telecommunication lines, often telephone lines, may be repeated and corrected. **Parity** is an error checking method.

The baud rate indicates the **bits** per second transmitted to the receiving computer. Baud rates are basically standardized. Options which may be used with this form of the Mode command are: 110, 300, 600, 1200, 2400, 4800, or 9600. Most personal computers use the 300 or 1200 baud rates, though 2400 is becoming more popular as the cost of 2400-baud modems drops.

There are three parity check options. There may be no error checking, or parity may be set as either even or odd. Data is communicated in blocks. Each block includes bits of data represented by binary digits. Their value is either zero (0) or one (1). If even parity checking is used, the parity bit is set to either 0 or 1 in order to make the value of the entire transmitted block "even." If parity is odd, the reverse happens. The receiving computer then checks the parity of each block of data received. If it does not match the parity, a message is sent to retransmit the last block of data.

Word length is set by the databit's size, i.e., either 7 or 8 bits. Those 7 or 8 bits represent a character. The receiving computer must know how long each "word" is. The computer's not knowing word length can be compared to your trying to reading a book without spaces between the words. You would find it frustrating, confusing, and difficult to interpret.

The syntax of this Mode command option is

MODE  COMn[:]b[,p][,d][,s][,T]

where n equals the serial port number (i.e., Com1: or Com2:), b is the baud rate, p represents parity, d is databits, and s is stopbits.

The options for parity, as discussed earlier, are

N          none
O          odd
E          even

Word length or databit size may be 7 or 8.  Stopbits are set to 1 or 2.

If the command were used to set baud rate as 300, parity at even, databits at 7, and stopbits at 1 using serial port #1 (i.e., Com port 1), the following command form would be appropriate:

MODE  COM1:12,E,7,1

The T parameter is used only when the asynchronous adapter is also being used for a serial printer.  It causes the computer to try again if **time-out** errors are encountered because the port is in-use by the printer.  The T parameter causes the system to keep looping until the port is free and data can be transmitted.

Most computer users involved in telecommunications use a **terminal software program**.  This type of software makes it easier for the user to set the communications protocol without using the Mode command.  You may never have to do more than select options from a terminal program menu, and the software then invokes the Mode command for you.


**THE MODE COMMAND:  SWITCHING FROM PARALLEL TO SERIAL**

The final option is to use Mode to switch output from a parallel port (i.e., Lpt1:  or Lpt2:  or Lpt3:) to a serial port (i.e., Com1:  or Com2:).  The command syntax is

MODE  LPTn[:]=COMm[:]

where n is the number of the parallel port and m represents the asynchronous port number.  Remember, the parallel port options are only 1, 2 or 3, while the serial port options are 1 or 2.

To send data output to serial port 2 instead of parallel port 1, the command form would be

MODE  LPT1:=COM2:

## GUIDED ACTIVITY:  THE PRINT MODE OPTION

All the Mode command forms are hardware-dependent, so it is difficult to present Guided Activities to demonstrate each option.  Therefore, this exercise will use only the Print option of the Mode command.  This activity assumes that a dot-matrix printer is attached to your microcomputer.  First you will set the printer output to condensed print (132 characters per line, 8 lines per vertical inch) and print a directory listing.  Then the activity will guide you in resetting the printer output to 80 characters per line with 6 lines per vertical inch.

1. Be sure the printer is turned on and the paper set to the top of the form.

2. Type **MODE LPT1:132,8**

3. Press <CR>.

The screen will return the following message:

LPT1:  set for 132
Printer lines per inch set

4. Type **DIR > PRN** and Press <CR>.

Check your printer and notice the condensed print size.

5. Type **MODE LPT1:80,6** and Press <CR>.

The monitor screen will respond with the message

Lpt1:  Set for 80

Printer lines per inch set

6. Type **DIR > PRN**

7. Press <CR>.

Check your printer and notice that the print size has returned to normal, i.e., 10 characters per inch.

**THE DOS VIRTUAL DISK**

Three types of disk drives are used with personal computers. The two most obvious ones are floppy disk drives and hard disks (sometimes referred to as fixed disks). Both of these types must be formatted first, and can then be used as secondary storage. Data may be stored including application program code, operating system code (DOS), and data, (text files, data base files, etc.).

The third type of disk is less tangible and less easily understood. It is the **virtual disk**. DOS 3.0 and above provides a file called VDISK.SYS which can be called from the configuration file (CONFIG.SYS) to create a **virtual drive**. Once created, a virtual drive can be treated as any other disk drive or hard disk, with a couple of exceptions:

1. virtual drives never need to be formatted before use;
2. virtual drives are volatile memory or storage.

A virtual disk is created from a portion of memory. Files may be copied to it or from it. However, when you reboot the computer or if the system loses power, any data stored on the virtual drive is lost.

Why are virtual drives used? A floppy drive is a slow method of transferring data to and from the CPU. It must get "up to speed" before data can be read. That takes milliseconds, which ultimately slow down the process time. A hard disk is faster, but is still a mechanical device. It operates faster than the floppy drive, but slower than a virtual drive. There are no mechanical parts to a virtual drive. It does not have to get up to speed. It operates at the speed of electrons. Any electronic device is faster than a mechanical device. Speed is what makes the virtual drive attractive.

The virtual drive is created in conjunction with the Device command and placed in the CONFIG.SYS file. To install the virtual drive, the following syntax is used.

Note that this command is not generated via the keyboard, but from the CONFIG.SYS file, which is read immediately after the resident portion of DOS is loaded and before the AUTOEXEC.BAT file is read.


    DEVICE = VDISK.SYS  [k]  [s]  [d][/e][:st]


where k is the size of the virtual drive in kilobytes, and s represents the number of **bytes** per sector on the virtual disk. The d parameter indicates the maximum number of directory listings contained on the virtual drive. One directory equates with one file. If you intend to have 12 files on the virtual drive, the directory parameter must be set to 12 or a larger number.

The /E parameter tells DOS to place the virtual drive in extended memory, i.e., memory above the 1-megabyte level. The :st parameter refers to the number of sectors transferred at one time from the virtual drive to the CPU.

This is important only if you are operating in extended memory. With a virtual disk in extended memory, the possibility exists that some interrupts may be lost. Interrupts are the way that hardware and software try to get the attention of the CPU. An interrupts says, "there's another task for the CPU to handle, stop what you are doing." Sometimes the number of sectors transmitted at one time must be reduced to minimize the length of time the transfer takes, because interrupts are being lost.

To create a virtual disk composed of 64 kilobytes, 128 byte sectors (transmitted 4 sectors at a time), and 32 directory entries in extended memory, the command form would be

    DEVICE=VDISK.SYS 64 128 32/E:4

When the virtual drive is installed, DOS issues the following message

    VDISK Version 2.0 virtual disk  x

where x is the drive designation of the virtual drive.  If your computer has two floppy disk drives, then DOS assigns the virtual drive as C:.  On the other hand, the virtual drive would become D:  if your system already has two floppy drives plus a hard disk.

**GUIDED ACTIVITY:  USING THE VIRTUAL DRIVE**

This exercise can only be completed with PC-DOS version 3.x or higher.  The Vdisk command is not available on earlier versions of PC-DOS.

In the Guided Activity, you will create a small (64K) virtual drive, then copy files to the drive.  You'll also graphically see that any data stored on a virtual drive is lost when the computer system looses power or is rebooted.  Drive C:  is used for the virtual drive in this exercise.  If your virtual drive has a different name, use it instead of C: throughout the exercise.

  1. Place the DOS diskette in drive A:.

  2. Insert your data diskette in the B: drive.

  3. Boot the system.

  4. Enter date and time when prompted.

  5. Type **EDLIN CONFIG.SYS**

  6. Press <CR>.

The screen will display the Edlin prompt as follows:

    New file
    *
    _

  7. Press <I> to insert text.

  8. Press <CR>.

 9. Type **DEVICE=VDISK.SYS 64 128 12**

10. Press <CR>.

11. Press <^C>.

The monitor display should appear as shown in Figure 9-1 below.

```
A:>EDLIN CONFIG.SYS
New file
*I

    1:*DEVICE=VDISK.SYS 64 128 12
    2:*^C

*_
```

FIGURE 9-1.  Screen Display When Creating CONFIG.SYS File


12. Press <E>.

13. Press <CR>.

14. To reboot your system, simultaneously press the <CTRL>, <ALT>, and <DEL> keys.

Assuming that you have a microcomputer system with two floppy disk drives, the message in Figure 9-2 will appear.  If you have one floppy drive, the virtual drive will be B:.  If you have two floppy drives plus a hard disk, the new virtual drive will be designated D:.

```
VDISK Version 2.0 virtual disk C:
     Buffer size:          64 KB
     Sector size:          128
     Directory entries:     12

Current date is Tue 1-01-1980
Enter new date (mm-dd-yy):
```

FIGURE 9-2.  Boot Message With Virtual Drive Installed

15. Enter date and time.

16. Type **DIR C:**

17. Press <CR>.

Figure 9-3 shows the screen response you should receive.

```
A:>DIR C:

   Volume in drive C is VDISK V2.0
   Directory of C:\

File not found

A:>
```

FIGURE 9-3.  Empty Directory Listing On Drive C:


Next you will copy three files created earlier in this Unit to the virtual drive.

18. Type **COPY B:*.* C:**

19. Press <CR>.

20. Type **C:**

21. Press <CR>.

22. Type **DIR**

23. Press <CR>.

The screen should resemble that shown in Figure 9-4, and display at least three files now on your virtual drive.

```
A:>C:

C:>DIR

   Volume in drive C is VDISK V2.0
   Directory of C:\

INPUTS           8      11-01-86         1:02p
FILELIST      1614      11-01-86        12:51p
FINDTEXT       251      11-01-86         3:25p
         3 File(s)      62208 bytes free

C:>
```

FIGURE 9-4.  Directory Listing Of Virtual Drive C:

At this point you could go in and edit one of the files using Edlin.  However, the Path command must first be used to open a pathway between the default drive (C:) and the drive with the Edlin external DOS command (A:).

24. Type **PATH A:**

25. Press <CR>.

26. Type **EDLIN FINDTEXT**

27. Press <CR>.

The screen will display the Edlin prompt and the following message:

    End of input file
    *
    ─

28. Press <L>.

29. Press <CR>.

Remember this text from an earlier exercise?  The monitor display will appear as shown in Figure 9-5.

```
C:>EDLIN FINDTEXT
End of input file
1*

        1:*This is a file in which to
        2: test the Find Filter provided
        3: by DOS 3.0 and higher.
        4:
        5: To test or not to test...
        6: that is not the question.
        7: Rather, the question is whether
        8: Find can find the word test
        9: or if the test will be failed.
       10:
       11: TEST PATTERN!
  *_
```

FIGURE 9-5.  Listing FINDTEXT File On Virtual Drive C:

You could edit this file, but instead just quit and exit.

30. Press <Q>.

31. Press <CR>.

32. When prompted :Abort edit (Y/N)?", Press <Y>.

33. To reboot your system, simultaneously press the <CRTL>, <ALT>, and <DEL> keys.  We will check to see if in fact the virtual drive data is volatile!

34. After the Power-On Self-Test concludes, the screen will indicate that the virtual drive is installed (see Figure 9-2).  Enter time and date when prompted.

35. Type **DIR C:**

36. Press <CR>.

The files are gone.  They did disappear when the warm boot turned the system off.

## BACKGROUND PRINTING WITH THE PRINT COMMAND

Printing a long document can tie up a microcomputer for several minutes, causing users to twiddle their thumbs until the tedious task is complete. Without special software or the Print command, you can get very frustrated. The Print command which first became available with DOS 2.x, helps relieve this problem.

The Print command creates a queue, or listing, of files to be printed to a specified printer. With the introduction of the Print command, PC-DOS took a step toward multitasking, i.e., handling more than one task at a time.

The Print command syntax, in its simplest form, is


PRINT  [d:][filename.ext]


The Print command has several optional parameters. The most common are listed below. The first three parameters are used only the first time the Print command is invoked in each computing session.

/D:device          Indicates to which serial or parallel port the printer is connected. The default device is PRN, i.e., Lpt1:.

/B:buffersize      Reserved memory (in bytes) for the Print command queue. The default size is 512 bytes.

/Q:queue-size      Specifies the number of files which may be queued at one time. The default value is 10 files.

/T                 Terminates the queue, i.e., cancels all files in the queue and stops printing. When printing is stopped, paper in the printer is advanced to the next top of the form.

/C                 Cancels selected files. The /C parameter is tacked onto the end of the filename. All files listed on the command line after this parameter are also cancelled until a /P is encountered.

/P                 Prints selected files and/or queues them for printing. The /P parameter is tacked onto the end of a filename on the command line. All files listed on the command line after this parameter are also queued for printing until a /C is encountered.

Upon booting your system, you would use the following command form to create a Print command queue to the serial port #1, and reserve 5120 bytes (5K) of memory for a queue which can handle 5 files:

    PRINT  /D:COM1:/B:5120/Q:5

The same size buffer for the Parallel port #1 would be generated by

    PRINT  /D:PRN/B:5120/Q:5
    or
    PRINT  /B:5120/Q:5

If the second form is used, DOS will prompt you for the "Name of list device". If you press the <ENTER> key, the default setting of PRN or Lpt1: will be assumed by DOS.

If three files named LETTER1.DOC, LETTER2.DOC, and LETTER3.DOC were to be printed, either of two command forms could be used. The first would list multiple filenames after the Print command

    PRINT  LETTER1.DOC LETTER2.DOC LETTER3.DOC

The other option would use global wildcard characters.

    PRINT  LETTER?.DOC

The /P parameter is assumed unless it follows a /C parameter on the same command line. In the above example, if a file LETTER4.DOC existed on the disk and should not be printed, the command could be modified to read

    PRINT  LETTER?.DOC LETTER4.DOC/C

Immediately after entering the above command, you could determine which files were active in the queue simply by entering:

    PRINT

The screen response shown in Figure 9-6 would appear.

```
A:>PRINT

A:LETTER1.DOC is currently being printed
A:LETTER2.DOC is in queue
A:LETTER3.DOC is in queue

A:>_
```

FIGURE 9-6.  Screen Response Indicating Status of Queue

All files in the queue, including the file currently being printed, could be cancelled by entering the command form

PRINT /T

There are several commands that can interfere with the Print command queue. They include any attempt to use the printer, such as redirecting the output of a DOS command to the printer port used by the Print command queue, or trying to use the PRTSC (print screen) key.

It is also important to avoid altering files in the queue until they have been completely printed and released from the queue.

The most effective use of the Print command is to print files to disk, thus saving any control characters used to format printed output.  Later the Print command can be used to queue several files for printing. While those files are printing, you can return to other computing tasks.

Some DOS commands slow down the printing process.  You will notice an appreciable slow-down in either the printing or the computing task.  This is because in a multitasking environment, one task is given priority over the other.  The high-priority task is said to run in the **foreground** while the low-priority task runs in the **background**.

We began this discussion by indicating that the Print command operates in the background because use of the command frees you to return to another application.  Thus it will appear that the Print command operates in the background--while you tackle another task in the foreground.  Technically, the reverse it true.  The Print command is really the high-priority task and runs in the foreground.  More important than which task runs in the foreground is that at least the Print command is a step in the right direction--toward making the IBM PC family of computers multitasking machines.

**GUIDED ACTIVITY:  CREATING A PRINT QUEUE**

In this Guided Activity, you will create several little text files using the Copy command.  Subsequently, you will use the Print command to queue the files for printing.

 1. Boot the system.

 2. Enter date and time when prompted.

 3. Type **B:**

 4. Press <CR>.

 5. Type **COPY FILELIST DIR1**

 6. Press <CR>.

 7. Type **COPY FILELIST DIR2**

 8. Press <CR>.

 9. Type **COPY FILELIST DIR3**

10. Press <CR>.

11. Type **COPY FILELIST DIR4**

12. Press <CR>.

13. Type **DIR DIR?**

14. Press <CR>.

The screen response should appear as shown in Figure 9-7.

```
B:>DIR DIR?

   Volume in drive B has no label
   Directory of B:\

DIR1        1614        11-01-86   12:51p
DIR2        1614        11-01-86   12:51p
DIR3        1614        11-01-86   12:51p
DIR4        1614        11-01-86   12:51p

     4 File(s)        350208 bytes free

B:>_
```

FIGURE 9-7.  DIR Listing of Copied Files

15. Be sure that your printer is turned on and the paper is set to the top of the form.

Next we must set up the **print queue**.

16. Type **A:**

17. Press <CR>.

18. Type **PRINT /D:PRN/B:5120/Q:4**

19. Press <CR>.

The screen display will appear as shown in Figure 9-8.

```
A:>PRINT /D:PRN/B:5120/Q:4
Resident part of PRINT installed
PRINT queue is empty

A:>_
```

FIGURE 9-8.  Screen Response To Setup of PRINT Command Queue

Now you will send the four newly created (copied) files to the queue.

**20. Type PRINT B:DIR?**

**21. Press <CR>.**

Your printer should begin printing out the text of the first file; the monitor should respond with the following message:

| | |
|---|---|
| B:DIR1 | is currently being printed |
| B:DIR2 | is in queue |
| B:DIR3 | is in queue |
| B:DIR4 | is in queue |

**22. Quickly, type PRINT B:DIR4/C to cancel the file named DIR4.**

**23. Press <CR>.**

The monitor screen will display a message indicating the status of files in the print queue. The file B:DIR4 should not appear, since the last command removed it from the queue. The message might look like the following, depending on how quickly you executed the command in step 23:

| | |
|---|---|
| B:DIR2 | is currently being printed |
| B:DIR3 | is in queue |

**24. If the printer is still running, type PRINT /T to terminate all files in the queue.**

**25. Press <CR>.**

The printing should cease and the screen should indicate that--

PRINT  queue is empty

## COMMAND REVIEW DICTIONARY

In this unit you have read about several DOS commands.  Most commands have optional parameters. We have tried to cover both the common and the rarely used forms of each command.  The following forms of this unit's commands are the most frequently used and should be reviewed carefully.

| | |
|---|---|
| DEVICE=VDISK.SYS 64 128 12 | When placed in the Config.sys file, creates a virtual disk composed of 64K with 128 byte sectors and a maximum of 12 directory entries. |
| MODE BW80 | Causes a color monitor to display a maximum of 80 characters per line across the screen in monochrome. |
| MODE BW40 | Causes a color monitor to display a maximum of 40 characters per line across the screen in monochrome. |
| MODE CO80 | Causes a color monitor to display a maximum of 80 characters per line across the screen in color. |
| MODE CO40 | Causes a color monitor to display a maximum of 40 characters per line across the screen in color. |
| MODE COM1:12,E,7,1 | Sets the serial port protocol to accept and transmit data at 1200 baud with even parity, 7 databits as the word length, and one stopbit. |
| MODE LPT1:132,8 | Causes output to a parallel printer to be printed 132 characters wide and 8 lines per vertical inch. |
| MODE LPT1:80,6 | Causes output to a parallel printer to be printed 80 characters wide and 6 lines per vertical inch. |
| MODE LPT1:=COM1: | Redirects output from parallel port one to serial port one. |
| PRINT/D:PRN/B:10240/Q:5 | Creates a print queue of 10240 bytes (10K) that directs output to printer port one (Lpt1:) and can hold a maximum of five files. |
| PRINT | After creating a print queue, this command generates a status report of files in the queue and those being printed. |
| PRINT/T | Cancels the printing of all files in the print queue. |

## REVIEW QUESTIONS

1. What are the four uses of the Mode command?

2. What are the four parameters used with the Mode command to set the communications protocol?

3. What is baud rate, and which rates are most common for personal computer users?

4. What is parity?  What does it do?

5. Why is databit size important to telecommunications?

6. What is a virtual disk?  How is it created?

7. What is the advantage of a virtual disk?

8. What disadvantages exist for a virtual disk?

9. Which has the slowest access time, a fixed disk, virtual disk, or floppy disk drive?  Which has the fastest access time?  Why?

10. What function does the Print command serve?

11. How can all files in a print queue be cancelled?

12. How can a single file in a print queue be cancelled?

13. If a standard device is not stated in the Print command, which device is assumed?

14. Can global wildcard characters be used in the Print command parameters?

15. What is the distinction between foreground and background computing tasks?  Is a Print command queue foreground or background?


## DOCUMENTATION RESEARCH

Read chapter 6 of the IBM DISK OPERATING SYSTEM Version 3.1 manual.  Also read the sections of chapter 7 dealing with the Mode, and Print commands, and the section on the VDISK.SYS file in chapter 4.

1. What does the /P parameter do on option 1 of the Mode command?

2. When BASIC initializes printer output, what values are used for characters per line and lines per vertical inch?

3. If you had both a monochrome and a color monitor both connected to a color graphics/display adapter, how would you switch from an 80-column monochrome display to a 40-column color display using the Mode command?

4. When setting communications protocol, what is the default parity setting for the Mode command?

5. When setting communications protocol, what is the default databits setting for the Mode command?

6. When setting communications protocol, what is the default stopbits setting for the Mode command?

7. When setting communications protocol, is there a default baud rate setting for the Mode command?

8. When using the Mode command to set the communications protocol, is there a shortcut to changing just one parameter, such as baud, and thus using defaults for the other parameters?  If so, how?

9. What is the minimum size in kilobytes of a virtual drive?

10. What is the maximum size in kilobytes of a virtual drive?

11. What is the default size of a sector (in kilobytes) on a virtual disk?

12. Based on the default value, how many files could be stored on a virtual drive?  Can this number be increased?  Decreased?  How?

13. Is it possible to install more than one virtual drive?  How?

14. What response is given by DOS if the /D, /B, or /Q parameters of the Print command are given a second time in a computing session?

15. What happens if the device listed in the Print command is not physically attached to the computer (i.e., no printer is connected to parallel port #1)?

16. What is the maximum value for the PRINT /Q parameter, i.e., the maximum number of files a queue can hold?

17. What message is given after the PRINT /T command form is entered?

18. What message is given after the PRINT /C command form is entered?

# APPLICATION

# D

## PART 1: RESETTING PRINTER OUTPUT WITH THE MODE COMMAND

In the previous unit we discussed four uses of the Mode command. One use of Mode is to adjust printer output. In this application, you will create a file and then use the Mode command to print it out in two type sizes.

A. Create a small text file using Edlin. It should be between 10 and 20 lines in length.

B. Use the Mode command to set the printer to 132 characters wide with 8 lines per vertical inch.

C. With the paper set to the top-of-the-form, print your file to the printer. Do not advance the paper when done printing.

D. Use the Mode command to set the printer to 80 characters wide with 6 lines per vertical inch.

E. Print your file. Both printings should appear on the same page.

F. Turn in the printed page to your instructor.

# UNIT

# 10

# THE SAFETY DOS COMMANDS

**SUPPLIES NEEDED**

The supplies that you will need for completing this unit are

1. IBM DISK OPERATING SYSTEM Version 3.1 manual;
2. DOS 3.1 diskette;
3. three blank diskettes.

**OBJECTIVES**

After completing this unit, you will be able to

1. define the key component in any disaster recovery plan;
2. define the use of the Backup and Restore commands in contrast to the Copy and Diskcopy commands;
3. list the different parameters appropriate to the Backup and Restore commands;
4. list the two primary copy-protection methods used by software manufacturers and comment on how they affect the use of the Backup and Restore commands;
5. list the three DOS commands that interfere with the Backup and Restore commands;
6. discuss the need for a periodic system backup;
7. define the use of the Attrib command;
8. list at least two uses of a write-protected file.

## IMPORTANT COMMANDS

The Important commands introduced in this unit are

1. Backup command;
2. Restore command;
3. Attrib command.

## ASSIGNMENTS

Place a check in front of the assignments for this unit.

1.____ Review and understand the following terms listed in the Computer Terms Dictionary (Appendix A): alternative processing strategies, Attrib, attribute byte, Backup, backup disks, boilerplate documents, copy-protection, disaster recovery plan, enterprise, hard-disk crash, manual backup systems, read-and-write, read-only, Restore, and write-protected.
2.____ Guided Activity: The Backup and Restore Process.
3.____ Guided Activity: The Partial Restore Process.
4.____ Guided Activity: Marking Files Read-Only with the Attrib Command.
5.____ Review Questions.
6.____ Documentation Research.

## HOW TO SMILE WHEN DISASTER STRIKES

Disaster recovery planning is a basic part of the planning process for any data processing center. Yet microcomputer users tend to ignore this aspect of implementation until after disaster strikes. The most common function in any **disaster recovery plan** is to conscientiously make periodic **backups**.

But it should be understood that a full-scale disaster recovery plan includes more than periodic backups. A body of literature exists on the subject, primarily evolving out of the mainframe data processing environment. A complete disaster recovery plan must include such topics as **alternative processing strategies**, testing, security, **manual backup systems**, cost effectiveness, and impact on the **enterprise** (business or department). Our scope of concern in this unit will center on backup systems as provided by PC-DOS and MS-DOS.

While everyone tends to agree that periodic backups are needed in any computing environment, the definition of "periodic" can be debated at great length. For some microcomputer users it can be a weekly backup. For other installations, anywhere from thrice weekly to twice daily may be appropriate.

Two additional factors enter into any backup strategy. First is the consideration of the kind of medium to be used. Microcomputer systems use several types of media, including tape, disk, or cartridge backup. The second consideration is whether to do a complete backup or to back up only modified files.

PC-DOS versions 3.20 and lower do not support disk-to-tape backups, so we'll limit the discussion to back ups on to floppy diskettes. With DOS 2.0 the backup process permits the backup of files from a hard disk to floppy diskettes only.

DOS 3.1 and higher adds the capability of backing up from

1. one diskette to another diskette;
2. a diskette to a hard disk;
3. one hard disk to another hard disk.

Users who purchase microcomputer tape backup systems receive software to facilitate backup to tape or cartridge, even though DOS does not provide that capability.


## WHY DISASTER MAY STRIKE

In unit 1 we discussed the care and handling of diskettes. From that discussion, it should be clear that floppy disks may go "bad" or be damaged. Even expert care can sometimes be voided by accidentally stacking books on a disk, spilling liquid on a disk, or dropping the disk on a dusty surface. A hard disk appears more protected. It is encased in a metal enclosure inside the PC's system unit. Unfortunately, anything mechanical will eventually wear down. A hard disk is no exception.

A **hard disk crash** is every user's greatest fear--yet every hard disk will crash. It is only a matter of time. The term hard disk crash means that the read-write head in the hard disk unit comes in destructive contact with the disk platters. A hard disk is composed of several rigid platters, not unlike a series of diskettes. When the head gouges or scratches the recording surface of a platter, data is lost and that area can no longer store data. If the damage occurs on the area reserved for track zero (where the directory and file allocation table reside), the hard disk becomes unusable.

What causes a hard disk crash or head crash? The main two causes are

1. the read-write head mechanically fails and bumps into the recording surface;
2. the system unit is jarred or moved while the read-write head is in motion, thus causing the head to damage the recording surface.

In normal operation, the read-write head floats over the recording surface. If the head physically comes in contact with the platter, damage occurs. The IBM Diagnostic diskette, which is provided with each new system unit, includes a program to park the head of a hard disk unit. Before a hard disk system unit is moved, the read-write head should be parked. The software moves the head to a position above the platters. In that position vibrations from moving the unit are less likely to cause damage.

All hard disk failures are not the result of a read-write head crash. Additional problems include:

1. damage from power surges;
2. damage from radio frequency interference (RFI);
3. damage from static electricity.

## THE DOS BACKUP COMMAND

The Copy and Diskcopy commands may be used if a backup is limited in scope. For instance, if all data is on a disk or two, either Copy or Diskcopy will work. Because the Diskcopy command is intended for floppy disk copying only, it cannot be used to back up files on a hard disk.

The Copy command, on the other hand, can be used to back up data from a hard disk. Two limitations exist for this type of back up.

1. A double-sided double-density diskette formatted under DOS 2.x or higher can only store 112 files in its directory. The AT formatted high-density diskette can handle 224 directory entries. Each file on the disk, the disk volume label, each subdirectory, and each hidden file count toward the file directory table limit.
2. A double-sided double-density diskette formatted under DOS 2.x or higher can only store 360K of data. An AT formatted high-density diskette can store 1.2 megabytes of data. Figure 10-1 shows the various disk types, sectors per track, number of directory entries and other diskette data.

When either of these limits is exceeded, the copying process terminates with the error message "insufficient disk space".

| Disk Type | Sectors | FAT Sectors | DIR Sectors | Directory Listings | Storage in Kilobytes |
|-----------|---------|-------------|-------------|--------------------|----------------------|
| 2S2D | 9 | 4 | 7 | 112 | 354 |
| 2S4D | 9 | 10 | 7 | 112 | 711 |
| 2S4D | 15 | 14 | 14 | 224 | 1185 |

FIGURE 10-1. Data on Various Diskette Types Including Number of FAT Sectors, Directory Listings, Directory Sectors, Sectors per Track and Data Storage Capacity.

The Copy command might still be useful if a strategy is developed which groups files with similar extensions or similar file specifications using global wildcard characters (Copy *.DOC, Copy *.WKS, Copy *.DBF, Copy LETTER??.*, etc.). This process obviously eliminates typing a separate Copy command line for each and every file on the disk. The schema reduces the number of commands issued to back up the entire system and if grouped properly would allow multiple diskettes to be used in the process. If the files are not grouped appropriately, you may run out of space on a given diskette halfway through copying a specified group of files. If that occurs, you must rethink the file groupings or go back and copy files one-by-one to the target disk.

Whenever backing up a hard disk or subdirectory requires more than 2-3 diskettes, the Copy command becomes an awkward substitute for the DOS Backup command. Backup is an external DOS command created specifically to handle hard-disk system backups. Because it is external, either the BACKUP.COM file from the DOS diskette must be available on the default drive, or the drive, and path to the BACKUP.COM command must be specified.

The syntax of the command is

BACKUP  s:[filename.ext]  t:[filename.ext]

where s: represents the source of files to be backed up and t: represents the drive on which the duplicate files will be created. In its simplest form, all files on drive a: may be backed up to a disk in drive B: by invoking this command.

BACKUP  A:*.*  B:

In this form, the Backup command creates a backup of files in only the current or specified directory. It does not automatically back up files in any other directory, nor in the subdirectories below the current or specified directory.

Four parameters or switches may be used with the Backup command:

| | |
|---|---|
| /A | Appends backed up files to files already on the **backup disk**. |
| /D:mm-dd-yy | Backs up files which have been modified after a stipulated date. |
| /M | Backs up all files modified since the last backup. |
| /S | Backs up all files in the current or designated directory plus all subdirectory files below the current or specified directory. |

The last switch facilitates the backup of an entire hard disk. If the cur- rent directory is the root directory, and the /S parameter is used, then every file in every directory or subdirectory on the fixed disk will be backed up. The form of the command would be

BACKUP  C:*.*  A:/S

If we sought to back up only files modified since the last backup, we could add one more switch.

BACKUP  C:*.*  A:/S/M

If this new form of the command is executed in the root directory, it will cause all directories and subdirectories to be searched for files modified since the last backup. Those files will then be placed on the backup disk. Whenever a file is backed up, one of the **attribute bits** in the directory table is marked to indicate that the process has taken place. If that file is subsequently modified, the flag is removed to indicate that no backup has taken place since the last modification. When using the "/M" parameter, DOS looks only for unmarked files, i.e., those not marked as backed up in their current form. Those files only are then transferred to the backup disk. During the transfer process, the file is then marked as having been backed up.

The date switch (/D) can be useful only if you seek to back up files created or modified either on or since a specified date. If a periodic backup program has been implemented, the data switch could be used by entering the day after the last backup. However, this procedure is really less efficient that using the "/M" parameter.

For in the situation in which all directories and subdirectories are to be searched, and files created or modified since 15 August 1986 are to be backed up, the command format would be

    BACKUP  C:*.*  A:/S/D:8-15-86

In each of the last three examples, we have assumed that the default drive is C: and the system is logged in the root directory. If the default directory were not the root directory, only files in the current directory and its subdirectories would be backed up. The represents the root directory, when it is combined with the "/S" parameter, it forces the backup process to begin in the root directory and proceed to back up each subdirectory on the disk. With the date option, the modified command would be:

    BACKUP  C:\*.*  A:/S/D:8-15-86

**BACKUP COMMAND ERROR CODES**

Any disaster recovery plan has as its foundation the backup of all files stored or used by the user. If those backups are faulty, the entire recovery plan is disastrously flawed. DOS provides the following five exit error codes to assist the operator in determining whether the Backup command has terminated successfully or unsuccessfully:

 0 Backup command completed normally
 1 DOS found no files to back up
 2 Due to file sharing conflicts, on a local area network (LAN), some files were not backed up
 3 Backup command was terminated by user (using <CTRL-BREAK> key combination)
 4 Terminated because of other error

The codes may be accessed by using the batch processing subcommand, If Errorlevel.

**WHAT TO DO AFTER THE CRASH**

The Backup command has a twin called **Restore**. After a hard-disk failure or any other disaster, the Restore command is used to transfer files from the backup disks to a new hard disk or reformatted disk. Restore is an external DOS command.

The syntax of the command is

RESTORE  s:  [t:][filename.ext]

where s:  is the drive containing the files to be restored and t:  is the target drive.

In its simplest form, a restoration of all files on backup disks in drive A:  to drive B:  would be accomplished with this command:

RESTORE  A:  B:*.*

The Restore command uses only two parameters or switches.

/P        Causes the Restore command to prompt you before it restores files that are marked **read-only** or have been modified since the last backup.  The prompt allows the user to choose to restore or not, whichever is most appropriate.
/S        Restores all files in the current or designated directory, plus all subdirectory files below the current or specified directory.

The files on the source diskette must have been placed there by the Backup command.  These commands are Siamese twins; they work only in conjunction with each other.

Here is another example using the /S switch.  Let's assume several points:

1. The source backup disks are in drive a:
2. We seek to restore files to the hard disk, drive C:
3. The default drive is the root directory on drive C:
4. Files are to be restored to all subdirectories under the root directory.

With these assumptions, the correct form of the command is

RESTORE  A:  C:*.*/S

If the default drive and current directory were anything other than those stipulated in the assumptions, the command would need to be revised to

RESTORE  A:  C:\*.*/S

The Restore command uses the same exit error codes outlined under the Backup command.

## CAVEATS TO THE DOS BACKUP AND RESTORE

The Backup command is not the same as the Copy command. Files created by the Backup command cannot be accessed or used until they have been restored. The Copy and Backup commands serve different purposes; they are not interchangeable.

Neither is the Backup command related to Diskcopy. The latter command will Format new diskettes before making its copy of the source diskette. Backup does not incorporate the Format command. Diskettes to be used with the Backup command must already be formatted and preferably labeled, (e.g., backup disk 01, backup disk 02, backup disk 03, etc.). The diskettes created via the Backup command must be numbered consecutively, because the Restore command requires that the restoration process use the diskettes in the same order in which they were created. Keep in mind that it will take 25 to 30 360K diskettes to back up each 10 megabytes of hard-disk storage.

> Trivia:  To be exact, each 360K diskette really holds only 254K of data storage space (after deducting the sectors for FAT and the directory table).  If you had exactly 10 megabytes of data on your hard disk, it would take 28.92655 diskettes to store that data.

The Backup command will erase all files off a diskette unless the "/A" switch is used.  This is cause for caution.  The backup diskettes should be clearly labeled as such.  Data on any diskette mistakenly used as a backup diskette will be lost.  Further, it is wise to have a minimum of two completely separate sets of backup diskettes.  Most seasoned computer users have been through the horrendous experience of having a read error on a hard disk, having a single set of backup diskettes, and finding the set flawed. The greater the number of backups, the greater the safety in case of disaster.

To maximize the chances of having a recent, usable set of backup diskettes requires greater redundancy. Redundancy requires that hardware, software and data be duplicated.  True redundancy in a microcomputer business setting would require:

1. a backup microcomputer available for each user if their original machine malfunctioned;
2. an archival set of program diskettes available to reinstall;
3. a recent, complete backup of all data created by the user.

## A TYPICAL BACKUP SCHEDULE

Figure 10-2 shows a typical backup schedule that uses multiple sets of backup diskettes plus partial and complete backups.  This particular schedule uses four sets of backup diskettes labeled A, B, C, and D.  C and D are only used for complete backups.  Sets A and B are used to back up modified files (in between each Friday full system backup).

In a typical office setting, the back up would only cover specific hard disk subdirectories containing data. If you have an archival set of program disks for your application programs, those files do not need to be backed up.  The original program disks or an archival copy provides the redundancy needed.

The schedule assumes that the "/S" parameter is used when needed to back up all subdirectories containing data.  The strategy follows these guidelines.

1. Make a full backup every Friday with alternating sets of diskettes.
2. Make a backup of modified files on Monday through Thursday.
3. The Monday and Tuesday backup of modified files does not use the "/A" parameter. This overwrites all files on the disk sets except files altered since the full backup on the previous Friday.
4. The Wednesday and Thursday backup of modified files uses the "/A" parameter. This adds additional altered files to disk sets A and B, respectively, yet preserves the modified files backed up on Monday and Tuesday.

| Monday | Tuesday | Wednesday | Thursday | Friday |
|---|---|---|---|---|
| | 1 Backup/M to set A | 2 Backup/M/A to set B | 3 Backup/M/A to set A | 4 Full Backup to set C |
| 7 Backup/M to set B | 8 Backup/M to set A | 9 Backup/M/A to set B | 10 Backup/M/A to set A | 11 Full Backup to set D |
| 14 Backup/M to set B | 15 Backup/M to set A | 16 Backup/M/A to set B | 17 Backup/M/A to set A | 18 Full Backup to set C |
| 21 Backup/M to set B | 22 Backup/M to set A | 23 Backup/M/A to set B | 24 Backup/M/A to set A | 25 Full Backup to set D |
| 28 Backup/M to set B | 29 Backup/M to set A | 30 Backup/M/A to set B | 31 Backup/M/A to set A | |

FIGURE 10-2. A Typical Full and Modified-Only Backup Schedule

Three DOS commands exist that can play havoc with the backup and restore process. The first two are Join and Subst, new DOS commands born with the advent of DOS version 3.1. They should never be invoked while the Backup or Restore commands are to be used. The third is Assign. Both Assign and Subst may confuse either DOS or the user on the true drive designation to be used in a backup and restore process. The Join command can confuse the tree structure, thus making it invalid after a backup and restore procedure.

There is one additional class of problem software which loves to decimate carefully planned and executed backups. It is the group of handy little memory-resident programs which includes clock display software, background communications programs, print spoolers, note pads, telephone dialers, screen-savers, and much more. These programs increase productivity, but may cause untold havoc when running concurrent with DOS's Backup and Restore commands. Memory-resident programs also cause problems with proprietary tape backup software such as utilized by the Tallgrass Technologies tape backup system. If getting ready to back up or restore your files, first reboot the system without loading any memory-resident programs!

One final caveat for the user. Although several major manufacturers have removed **copy-protection** from their software, the nuisance remains on some software. To understand the impact on backup procedures, it is important to understand how copy-protection works. On a non-copy-protected disk, the DOS Diskcopy command creates a duplicate disk by reading each track in sequence and copying the date to the corresponding track on the source disk. The Copy command copies a file sector by sector (or cluster by cluster) from one disk to another. With the Copy command there is no guarantee that the file will be stored on the target disk at the same physical location, the same track or sector, as the file occupied on the source diskette.

Copy-protection thwarts copying by any one of a number of methods, including rearranging the order in which the tracks are recorded, recording between tracks, recording tracks backward, using spiral rather than concentric tracks, and deliberately writing or creating bad sectors that must exist in specific locations before the disk is readable.

Typically, two methods of copy-protection persist:

1. use of a key diskette;
2. use of an install procedure that permits a limited number of installs of copy-protected files.

Manufacturers using the first copy-protection method keep all the "protected" files on the key diskette. The key diskette must be in one of the floppy disk drives for the copy-protected software to work. With this scheme, the files to be placed on a hard disk are typically not copy-protected. This method does not affect the use of the Backup and Restore commands, unless you attempt to backup and restore the key diskette.

The latter method installs "protected" files on the hard disk. These files cannot be copied using the DOS Copy, Diskcopy, or Backup commands. In essence, if you have backed up your files and the hard disk crashes, there is no way to restore the copy-protected files from the backup disks. Because a limited number of installs are allowed, usually one or two, a hard-disk crash means you have lost one install. After a hard-disk failure, only two options exist: try to uninstall the copy-protected programs (often not a real possibility) or contact the software manufacturer and appeal to their mercy.

The point of this discussion? Do not expect the Backup and Restore commands to provide a usable disaster recovery system for copy-protected software. In fact, you can anticipate an 80% chance that trying to back up or restore copy-protected software will blow your the software away. One popular software program recently eliminated copy-protection--but only after numerous complaints from users. The copy-protection scheme caused the program diskette to automatically erase if the hidden files were flagged by using the DOS Backup command.

## BACK UP: A WEARISOME EXERCISE

One of the dreariest tasks for most computer users is backing up files. It is tedious to use the DOS Backup and Restore commands. Other vendors have entered the arena with software products which provide a speedier backup than the standard DOS commands. Further, tape backup systems tend to reduce user interaction in the backup process. Rather than swapping from 25 to 30 diskettes in and out of the drive to back up 10 megabytes of data, a tape backup system stores that much data on one tape. Some systems, like the TG-4060 produced by Tallgrass Technologies of Lenexa, Kansas, can store up to 60 megabytes of data on one tape.

There are options for the microcomputer user beyond what is offered by MS-DOS and PC-DOS. However, whichever system is used, the crucial guideline is that periodic backups are essential. Backups should occur as often as dictated by the maxim, "back up everything you cannot afford to lose!". If you cannot afford to lose a day's work, then your backup should be done at least daily. Don't let a tedious task deter you from having the security of a complete system backup.

## GUIDED ACTIVITY:  THE BACKUP AND RESTORE PROCESS

In this Guided Activity, you will use the Backup and Restore commands to create a backup of your data diskette, and subsequently restore the files to a second disk.

This activity can only be accomplished if you have access to DOS version 3.x. Earlier versions do not permit back up from one diskette to another.

One caution--the Backup and Restore commands do not like memory-resident programs. That includes keyboard enhancers, calculators, notepads, etc. Even memory-resident programs such as screen-savers (blank the screen after a predefined time period) will play havoc with Backup and Restore. Be sure that no memory-resident programs are present before you begin this exercise.

1. Place the DOS 3.1 disk in drive A:.

2. Boot the computer.

3. Enter date and time when prompted.

4. Type **FORMAT B:**

5. Press <CR>.

6. When prompted, insert a blank diskette in drive B:. Use one of the new unformatted diskettes; do not use your data disk from previous exercises.

7. Press <CR>.

8. When prompted "Format Another (Y/N)," Press <Y>.

9. Press <CR>.

10. When prompted, remove the newly formatted disk from drive B: and label it BACKUP DISK 01, then insert second blank diskette in drive B:.

11. Press <CR>.

12. When prompted "Format Another (Y/N)," Press <Y>.

13. Press <CR>.

14. When prompted, remove the second newly formatted disk from drive B: and label it PARTIAL BACKUP DISK 01, then insert third blank diskette in drive B:.

15. Press <CR>.

16. When prompted "Format Another (Y/N)," Press <N>.

17. Press <CR>.

18. Remove the third newly formatted disk from drive B: and label it NEWDOS DISK 01.

You should now have available three formatted blank diskettes, the data diskette from the previous exercises, and the DOS 3.1 diskette.

19. Type **BACKUP A:*.* B:**

20. Press <CR>.

21. When prompted to "Insert backup source diskette," simply leave the DOS data diskette in drive A:.

22. Press any key.

23. When prompted to "Insert backup diskette 01," place the blank disk labeled BACKUP DISK 01 in drive B:.

Notice the screen warning that "Files in the target drive B:\ root directory will be erased".

24. Press any key.

The screen should echo the following message:

> \*\*\* Backing Up Files To Drive B: \*\*\*
> Diskette Number: 01

Then the files contained on the DOS diskette, beginning with the hidden files IBMBIO.COM and IBMDOS.COM, will be listed as they are backed up to drive B:.

25. When the DOS prompt appears again (i.e., A>), type **DIR B:/P**

Note that the first file listed on your backup disk is BACKUPID.@@@. This file simply stores the volume number (i.e., 01), of the backup diskette.

26. Press any key to finish the directory listing.

27. Remove the DOS diskette from drive A: and insert BACKUP DISK 01.

28. Do a warm boot by simultaneously pressing <CTRL>, <ALT>, and <DEL> keys.

The backup disk has all the files contained on your DOS diskette yet it will not boot. The monitor will display the following message:

> Non-system disk or disk error
> Replace and strike any key when ready

Remember that the Backup command creates a mirror image that is readable only by the Restore command.

29. Remove the BACKUP DISK 01 and insert the DOS diskette in drive A:

30. Strike any key and DOS will load.

31. Enter date and time when prompted.

32. Type **RESTORE A: B:\*.\***

33. Press <CR>.

34. When prompted to "Insert backup diskette 01," place the BACKUP DISK 01 in the A: drive.

35. Press any key.

36. When prompted to "Insert restore target" diskette, place the newly formatted NEWFILE DISK 01 in drive B:.

37. Press any key.

The screen message shown in Figure 10-3 will appear, followed by a list of all the files on the backup disk. As the files are restored, they are listed on the screen.

```
    *** Files were backed up MM/DD/YY drive A: ***

    *** Restoring files from drive A: ***
    diskette 01:
            \IBMBIO.COM
            \IBMDOS.COM
            \ANSI.SYS
            \ASSIGN.COM
```

FIGURE 10-3.  Screen Response When Using Restore Command

When the restore process concludes, you will hear a beep and see the following message:

    System files restored
    Target disk may not be bootable

38. When the DOS prompt reappears, remove the BACKUP DISK 01 from drive A: and insert the disk labeled NEWDOS DISK 01 into that drive.

39. Do a warm boot by simultaneously pressing the <CTRL>, <ALT>, and <DEL> keys.

If the backup and restore process was successful, your system will reboot and you'll be prompted to enter the date and time.

## ADDITIONAL NOTES ON RESTORE

A few supplemental notes on the Restore command may be helpful.  First, a single file or group of files may be restored using the Restore command.  Even though the previous Guided Activity focused on a total restoration of files, you can select the option of partially restoring from one or more backup diskettes.

In the previous exercise, the BACKUP DISK 01 includes the FORMAT.COM file.  That single file could be restored by using the command line

     RESTORE A: B:FORMAT.COM

Groups of files may be restored using the DOS wildcard characters.  If our backup diskette included an assortment of worksheet files (.WS extension), backup worksheet files (.BWS extension), text files (.TXT extensions), and document files (.DOC extension); a partial restoration of all document files could be accomplished using the command line

     RESTORE A: B:*.DOC

The Restore command has a minor idiosyncrosy related to subdirectories.  If you have organized your hard disk (or a floppy disk) into subdirectories, you can only restore files to the subdirectory from which they were originally backed up.  This is really a minor disadvantage in most cases.  However, if you were switching from a ten megabyte hard disk to a twenty megabyte drive and wished to re-organize the subdirectories on the new drive, the process is awkward.  You would need to:

1. back up the 10 megabyte hard disk,
2. remove the 10 megabyte drive and replace it with the 20,
3. restore all files to the 20 megabyte drive into the same subdirectories they occupied on the old drive,
4. create the new subdirectory structure,
5. copy files into the new subdirectories,
6. delete files from the old directories and
7. remove old directories which are empty of files.

One nice feature--the Restore command will recreate subdirectories if they were lost due to accidental erasure, or when switching to a new hard disk.  If the subdirectory existed when the backup was made, and does not exist on the target drive, the subdirectory(s) will be recreated during the restoration process.

One final note:  under certain circumstances, the Backup command provided in DOS version 2.x will substituted a hexidecimal 0 for one of the filename characters on the target diskette.  This error produces a set of flawed backup diskettes that will not work with the Restore command.  Thus, the time and effort used to back up data is wasted--because the data cannot be restored.  This bug was cured with the new DOS 3.x version Backup command--which is a good reason by itself for users to upgrade to DOS 3.x.

## GUIDED ACTIVITY:  THE PARTIAL RESTORE PROCESS

This activity is a follow-up to the preceding one.  Please complete the preceding Guided Activity, at least through step 31 before continuing.  During this activity, you will restore several executable (.EXE) files to a blank, formatted disk.

If continuing directly from the preceeding Guided Activity, begin with Step 40 (the NEWDOS DISK 01 should still be in drive A:). Otherwise, boot your system with a DOS 3.1 diskette in drive A: then proceed.

40. Enter date and time when prompted.

41. Type **RESTORE A: B:*.EXE**

This form of the command will restore from the backup disks all files ending with the .EXE extension.

42. Press <CR>.

43. When prompted to "Insert backup diskette 01 in drive A:," first remove NEWDOS DISK 01 and then place BACKUP DISK 01 in drive A:.

44. Strike any key.

45. When prompted to "Insert restore target" diskette, place the PARTIAL BACKUP 01 diskette in drive B:.

46. Strike any key.

The monitor screen will appear as shown in Figure 10-4.  These six files are the only .EXE files on the DOS 3.1 diskette.

```
*** Files were backed up MM/DD/YY drive A: ***

*** Restoring files from drive A: ***
diskette 01:
        \ATTRIB.EXE
        \FIND.EXE
        \JOIN.EXE
        \SHARE.EXE
        \SORT.EXE
        \SUBST.EXE

A>
```

FIGURE 10-4.  Screen Response When Completing Partial Restore

47. Type **B:**

48. Press <CR> to select the B: drive as the default drive.

49. Type **DIR**

50. Press <CR>.

Notice that the six files listed below are now on the disk in the B: drive:

ATTRIB.EXE
FIND.EXE
JOIN.EXE
SHARE.EXE
SORT.EXE
SUBST.EXE

The files are already in alphabetical order.  To determine if the restoration process was successful, you should attempt to use one of the DOS commands on the disk.  The easiest selection is the Sort command.  The next step uses Sort in conjunction with the internal Dir command to generate a reverse alphabetical order listing of files on the disk.

51. Type **DIR|SORT/R**

52. Press <CR>.

The files should be listed in this order.


      SUBST.EXE
      SORT.EXE
      SHARE.EXE
      JOIN.EXE
      FIND.EXE
      ATTRIB


Notice that with DOS 3.1 two additional files exist on the disk. These files have names like 000E150C or 0E2B310D. They are the temporary files used by the Sort command to organize the sorted items. These mystery files were discussed in an earlier unit.


## ANOTHER SAFETY COMMAND: ATTRIB

Microsoft Corporation added another safety feature with PC-DOS 3.x. It is the **Attrib** command. When a file is created on disk, a directory entry is also created. The eleventh byte of each directory entry is the attribute byte. Each bit composing the eleventh byte has a special meaning. The first bit indicates whether the file is read-only or marked for both **read-and-write** operations. This bit can be altered, changed from a 0 to 1, or vise-versa by using the external DOS command, Attrib. The command's syntax is


    ATTRIB [+R] or [-R][d:][filename.ext]


If we wish to **write-protect** (i.e., make read-only), a file on drive B: named JUNKMAIL.TXT, the attribute bit must be set to a value of 1. Therefore, the command takes the form of


    ATTRIB +R B:JUNKMAIL.TXT


After setting the attribute to read-only, we can determine that the process was successful by entering the command


    ATTRIB B:JUNKMAIL.TXT

DOS will respond with the message

    R       B:\JUNKMAIL.TXT

If the file's attribute were set to a read-and-write state, then the message would be

    B:\JUNKMAIL.TXT

The "R" appearing at the left margin indicates that the file is read-only or write-protected. The read-only attribute may be reset to 0, thus changing the file to a read-and-write state, by using the following command form

    ATTRIB -R B:JUNKMAIL.TXT

Global wildcard characters may be used with the Attrib command; thus, a group of files may be write-protected by a single command.

It is important to realize that any file which is write-protected using the Attrib command may be accessed and viewed. However, no modifications may be made to the file without changing the attribute bit to 0, i.e., not write-protected. This means that the Attrib command is useful only with files saved primarily for archival purposes. Files that are modified daily are not good candidates for the Attrib command.

The Attrib command would be useful in storing **boilerplate documents** for a word processor. If a department, company, or any enterprise finds that a basic response, with minor modifications, meets the needs of most correspondence they receive, then a series of standard paragraphs may be created and stored as a separate file. When needed, the file is copied into correspondence to clients. Once a file with the Attrib set to read-only is copied, the duplicate copy is not write-protected. Modifications and additions may be made to the new file, yet the boilerplate file remains intact and write-protected.

The same process could be used with generic worksheets created by a spreadsheet program. A standard worksheet is created to store monthly telephone traffic in a department. The file, MASTPHON.WS, is then write-protected using the Attrib command. Each month a new copy of the master file is created by using the command

    COPY MASTPHONE.WS PHONEJUL.WS

Our example shows the command format for the month of July. Subsequent files created for subsequent months might be named PHONEAUG.WS, PHONESEP.WS, PHONEOCT.WS, etc. Because the new files are copied, they lack the read-only attribute of the MASTPHONE.WS file.

An added feature of the Attrib command relates to the erasing of files. A file marked as read-only by the Attrib command cannot be erased using either the Del or Erase commands. However, the Format command will eliminate read-only files.

For addition discussion of the attribute byte in each file directory listing, refer to Unit 12 (Extended DOS Features).

**GUIDED ACTIVITY: MARKING FILES READ-ONLY WITH THE ATTRIB COMMAND**

In this exercise, you will create a small file using Edlin, mark that file as read-only, copy it several times, and then delete all but the file marked by the attribute byte as read-only. This will demonstrate that when a file marked as read-only is copied, the copy is not write-protected; and that a file marked as read-only cannot be deleted.

Because the ATTRIB command was first available with DOS 3.x, readers using earlier versions of DOS will be unable to complete this Guided Activity.

1. Insert DOS disk in drive A:.

2. Boot the computer system.

3. When prompted, enter date and time.

4. Type **EDLIN B:MASTER.WS**

5. Press <CR>.

6. When the Edlin prompt (i.e., asterisk) appears, press <I>

7. Press <CR>.

8. Type **Let's pretend this is a master copy**

9. Press <CR>.

10. Type **of a budget worksheet**

11. Press <CR>.

12. Type **created by our favorite electronic**

13. Press <CR>.

14. Type **spreadsheet program.**

15. Press <CR>.

16. Press <^C>.

17. Press <L> and press <CR> to verify that the copy is correct.  It should read:


Let's pretend this is a master copy
of a budget worksheet
created by our favorite electronic
spreadsheet program.


18. Press <E> to exit and save the file.

19. Press <CR>.

20. Type **ATTRIB +R B:MASTER.WS**

21. Press <CR>.

The file is now write-protected and marked as read-only by the Attrib command.  The next step will verify that MASTER.WS is write-protected.

22. Type **ATTRIB B:MASTER.WS**

23. Press <CR>.

The screen message should read


    R       B:\MASTER.WS


The R in the left-hand margin indicates that the attribute byte is set to read-only.  To reconfirm that the MASTER.WS is protected from modification, try to edit it using Edlin.

24. Type **EDLIN B:MASTER.WS**

25. Press <CR>.

The screen will return with the message


    File is READ-ONLY


The next few steps will create duplicates of the MASTER.WS file under four different filenames.

26. Type **COPY B:MASTER.WS B:JUNE86$$.WS**

27. Press <CR>.

28. Press <F2>.

29. Press <N>.

You will see that the function keys used for editing in Edlin operate the same way at the DOS level.

30. Type **LY** and press <F3>.

31. Press <CR>.

32. Press <F2>.

33. Press <J>.

34. Type **AUG**

35. Press the <DEL> key.

36. Press <F3>.

37. Press <CR>.

38. Press <F2>.

39. Press <A>.

40. Press <F2> again.

41. Press <A> again.

42. Type **SEP**

43. Press <F3>.

44. Press <CR>.

Check to be sure that the newly created files are on the B: drive disk.

45. Type **DIR B:**

46. Press <CR>.

The following files should be on the disk:

```
MASTER.WS
JUNE86$$.WS
JULY86$$.WS
AUG86$$.WS
SEP86$$.WS
```

The MASTER.WS file is read-only, but what about the files copied from it?

47. Type **EDLIN B:JUNE86$$.WS**

48. Press <CR>.

49. When the "End of input file" message appears, press <L>.

50. Press <CR>.

The text file should appear as shown in Figure 10-5 below.

```
        1: Let's pretend this is a master copy
        2: of a budget worksheet
        3: created by our favorite electronic
        4: spreadsheet program.
```

FIGURE 10-5.  Screen Display When Listing File in Edlin

In the next few steps, you will do a slight modification on the file.

51. Press <1>.

52. Press <CR>.

53. Press <F2> and press <M>.

54. Type **copy**

55. Press <CR>.

56. Press <L>.

57. Press <CR>.

The text file should now appear as shown in Figure 10-6 below.

```
   1: Let's pretend this is a copy
   2: of a budget worksheet
   3: created by our favorite electronic
   4: spreadsheet program.
```

FIGURE 10-6.  Screen Display of Exercise Text

Notice that the word "master" from line 1 is gone.

58. Press <E> to exit and save the file.

59. Press <CR>.

60. Type **DIR B:**

61. Press <CR>.

Notice that the file JUNE86$$.WS is now only 112 bytes long rather than 119 bytes long, i.e., the length of MASTER.WS.  In addition a new file, automatically created by DOS and titled JUNE86$$.BAK, has been created.  You were definitely able to modify the copy of a read-only file--even though the original was write-protected.

Finally, to assure you that read-only files cannot be deleted, the next few steps will attempt to do just that!

62. Type **DEL B:*.WS** This command will delete all files on drive B:  that end with the .WS extension.

63. Press <CR>.

64. Type **DIR B:**

65. Press <CR>.

Of the files created in this exercise, only two remain:

MASTER.WS
JUNE86$$.BAK

Clearly, the file marked as read-only withstood the Del command and is still safely available to you.

## COMMAND REVIEW DICTIONARY

In this unit you have read about several DOS commands. Most commands have optional parameters. We have tried to cover both the common and the rarely used forms of each command. The following forms of this unit's commands are the most frequently used and should be reviewed carefully.

| | |
|---|---|
| ATTRIB +R Filename | Marks the specified file as read-only. |
| ATTRIB -R Filename | Marks the specified file as read-and write accessible. |
| BACKUP C:\*.* A:/S | Backs up all files from all directories and subdirectories on hard disk C: to a floppy disk in the A: drive. |
| BACKUP C:*.* A:/M | Backs up all modified files (since the last backup) in the current directory of hard disk C: to a floppy disk in the A: drive. |
| RESTORE A: C:\*.*/S | Restores all files from the backup diskettes in drive A: to the appropriate directory or subdirectory on hard disk C:. |
| RESTORE A: C:Filename | Restores the specified file from the backup disk in drive A: to the hard disk C:. |

## REVIEW QUESTIONS

1. How are the uses of the Copy and Diskcopy commands different from the uses of the Backup and Restore commands?

2. Name at least three concerns the user should be aware of when using the Backup and Restore commands.

3. Which DOS commands should never be in effect when using the Backup or Restore commands?

4. What are the two primary methods used for copy-protecting application software? What impact does each have on the backup and restore process?

5. What is a disadvantage of the DOS Backup and Restore commands in comparison to tape backup systems?

6. What purpose does the Attrib command serve?

7. Why would globally changing all files to read-only not be wise?

8. Give an example of when write-protecting a file with the Attrib command would be useful.

## DOCUMENTATION RESEARCH

Refer to the IBM DISK OPERATING SYSTEM version 3.1 manual to answer the following questions. Read the portion of chapter 7 covering the Backup and Restore commands.

1. What is the difference between files created with the Backup command and those created with the Copy command?

2. If you are sharing files on a network and attempt to back up files to which you do not have access privilege, what message will be generated on the monitor screen?

3. Must backup diskettes be formatted before use with the Backup command?

4. If the target of the Backup command is a fixed disk, where will the files be stored?

5. Should the source diskette ever be write-protected when using the Backup command?  Explain your answer.

# APPLICATION

## PART 1: RESTORING AN ASCII TEXT FILE

In the previous unit we discussed the DOS commands to back up and restore program and data files. In this application, you will restore a file which was created earlier with the DOS Backup command.

A. Obtain a copy of the file "Message.txt" from your instructor. This file is **not** a regular text file. It is a backup file created with the Backup command.

B. Restore the file.

C. Once restored, redirect the file to a printer.

D. Turn in a printed copy of the file to your instructor.


## PART 2: SAFEGUARDING FILES WITH THE ATTRIB COMMAND

In this Application, you will create a small ASCII text file using Edlin and then mark it as a read-only file.

A. Create a small text file using Edlin. It should be between 10 and 20 lines in length.

B. Use the appropriate DOS command to mark the file as read-only.

C. Double check your work.  Try to delete the file.  If it cannot be deleted, you have correctly given the file the read-only attribute.

D. Turn in the file to your instructor on a diskette.

# UNIT

# 11

# DOS AND THE LOCAL AREA NETWORK

**SUPPLIES NEEDED**

The supplies that you will need for completing this unit are

1. IBM DISK OPERATING SYSTEM version 3.1 manual

**OBJECTIVES**

After completing this unit, you will be able to

1. define local area network (**LAN**);
2. discuss the causes behind the development of LANs;
3. discuss the advantages of a LAN;
4. define some issues related to selection of a LAN;
5. define and explain the purposes of DOS 3.x commands which support networks.

**IMPORTANT COMMANDS**

The important commands introduced in this unit are

1. Lastdrive
2. Share command;
3. Rcbs command.

## ASSIGNMENTS

Place a check in front of the assignments for this unit.

1.____ Review and understand the following terms listed in the Computer Terms Dictionary (Appendix A): cabling, CONFIG.SYS, disk server, file control block, file server, file-sharing, footprint, gateway, local area network, media, network administrator, node, and topology.
2.____ Review Questions.
3.____ Documentation Research.

## LOCAL AREA NETWORKS: THE WAVE OF THE FUTURE?

1986 was heralded as the year of the **local area network** (LAN). Though the adoption of a uniform standard for networks failed to materialize, manufacturers of LAN-related hardware and software made great strides forward. With the appearance of PC-DOS 3.x, IBM provided support via the operating system for such a system.

Before describing the commands in DOS 3.x which support networking, a working definition of a LAN and a discussion of the market forces which created a need for the LAN, are appropriate.

In the simplest form, a LAN is a hard-wired system connecting multiple work stations (i.e., microcomputers). A LAN facilitates the sharing of data, files, and peripherals. Originally LANs were contrasted with wide area networks, which used telecommunications to connect work stations. The systems are not as distinct today; a LAN may include hard-wired or cable linkages as well as linkages via modem.

Why did the LAN evolve? Personal computers gave new-found freedom to end users. With the greater variety of application software, tasks that had previously been handled by the data processing department were now performed at each worker's desk. But even before the euphoria faded, it became clear that data on an isolated work station could not conveniently be transported to another work station.

Workers at different work stations often needed to use the same data base or the same spreadsheets. To share data, files had to be copied to disk and transported to another work station before they could be used. Soon it became unclear which machine had the most recent, modified version of the file. Time was lost determining which version was accurate. Ultimately, there had to be a better way of sharing files. The LAN served that purpose. Shared files were stored either on a **file server** or a **disk server**. A file server is a hard-disk reserved specifically for shared files on the network. It is a separate and distinct resource on the network. A **disk server** is a hard-disk in one user's PC which is linked into the system for shared access by anyone on the network. A disk server is less expensive to implement than a dedicated file server, but access speed is slower.

A contributing factor was the high cost of peripherals. If a department had three work stations, each sought access to a printer. If the work required only a dot-matrix printer, the cost was not terribly restrictive, but if each work station needed access to true letter-quality reproduction, then the cost of peripherals skyrocketed. Further, if both graphics and letter-quality type were needed then each work station required two printers, a dot-matrix and a letter-quality. A recent alternative is the laser printer, but even with recent price drops the cost is in the $2,000 to $3,500 range. A related factor was the additional **footprint** (i.e., work space) required to handle a computer, two printers, and other necessary peripherals.

The LAN solved this problem by permitting users to access any printer or peripheral networked into the system. Thus a single laser printer or a single letter-quality printer could meet the needs of a department or enterprise.

A complete discussion of LANs cannot be covered in a single chapter. The installation of a network is not a simple matter. A few topics related to network selection include:

1. **Topologies**: How are the work stations connected? The standard topologies include token ring (adopted by IBM), star, and bus.
2. **Cabling**: What type of cable or **media** is to be used? This relates to the speed at which data can be communicated across the LAN. Types include twisted pair, baseband coaxial, and broadband coaxial.
3. Security: Will the system be password-protected? Can volumes or disk volumes be declared public or private?
4. Software: Are there network versions of the software to be used on the system?
5. Peripherals: What hardware can be shared via the network? Who should have access to the equipment? Does the system permit the restriction of certain peripherals to designated users?

Other issues might include: Will an electronic mail system be included? Do the network linkages require hardware and software, or just software? Who will serve as **network administrator** for the LAN; i.e., assign passwords, monitor usage, provide technical support? Is there a limitation on the distance between **nodes** (i.e., work stations) on the system? Will the system include a **gateway** (i.e., access to the enterprise's mainframe system)?

**NETWORK SUPPORT OFFERED BY PC-DOS 3.x**

DOS 3.1 provided disk, directory, and printer support for most DOS commands on several LANs, including the IBM PC-Net and Microsoft's MS-NET. With DOS 3.2, specific support features for IBM's token ring network were added. Each of the currently available versions of DOS 3.x provide three new commands specifically supporting networks. The commands are Share, Fcbs, and Lastdrive.

**THE SHARE COMMAND**

The Share command performs a straightforward function. It loads support for **file-sharing**. Three factors are controlled, including the number of files which may be open at one time, the number of locks, and the allocation of space for recording data necessary for file-sharing. When the Share command is activated, it checks the **file control block** (FCB) table. The FCB table is created by using the Fcbs command within the **CONFIG.SYS** file. CONFIG.SYS is always referenced when the computer system is booted.

Let us examine the Share command further.  The simplest form of the command is


SHARE


Since Share is an external command, the user must be logged-on to the drive and directory which includes the SHARE.EXE command file, or specify the drive and path prior to the command.  The following example assumes that the SHARE.EXE file is on drive C:  in the DOS subdirectory but the default drive is not C:.  This form also uses two default settings for the command.


C:\DOS\SHARE


If the default settings are not appropriate, then parameters must follow the command.  The two parameters or switches are

/F:bytesize          This switch sets the file size for a special file which stores data necessary for file-sharing.  For each file to be opened, the special file must be 11 bytes long plus the length of the full filename.  The default is 2048 bytes.
/L:locks             This switch allocates space for the number of locks desired.  The default size is for 20 locks.

If we spelled out the default settings in the Share command, it would be entered via the keyboard as


C:\DOS\SHARE/F:2048/L:20


The Share command need be invoked only once each time the system is booted.  If it is invoked a second time, DOS will issue a message stating "Share already installed."


## THE FILE CONTROL BLOCK COMMAND

The second network-related command is the Fcbs (file control block) command.  It is always used within the CONFIG.SYS file and follows the form


FCBS=m,p


where m equals the maximum number of files which may be open at one time and p equals the protected number of files.

If no Fcbs command is entered, DOS assumes the following default values:

FCBS = 4,0

which indicates that a maximum of four files may be open and that none of them are protected.  If the Share command is invoked, and you have specified Fcbs=4,0 in the CONFIG.SYS file, DOS automatically adjusts the FCB table to 16,8.  By examining this situation, we can better understand how the Fcbs command works.

That new default, created after Share was invoked, is the same as entering the following command in the CONFIG.SYS file:

FCBS = 16,8

If an application program opens 16 files during the course of its processing, the limit is not exceeded and all processing continues.  However, if subsequently the application needs to open one or more files, a dilemma ensues.  DOS has been told not to open more than 16 files, but the application is greedy for number 17.  DOS then surveys the files in use to determine the least recently used and proceeds to boot that file out of memory to make room for the new file, with one exception.  Because of the Fcbs command, the first 8 files loaded into memory are exempt from getting the boot, even if they would otherwise be the least recently used files.  A few guidelines are in order.

1. In the Fcbs command, the maximum number of files open (m) should never be exceeded by the number of protected (p) files.
2. If the maximum number of files (m) equals the number of protected files (p), then an error message will appear stating "FCB unavailable Abort, Retry, Ignore," and processing will cease.
3. If two or more FCBs refer to the same file on a network, then DOS counts the multiple FCBs as only one.
4. If an application experiences critical errors because of FCB files being closed, the maximum number of files (m) which may be open at one time is simply increased.
5. Whenever the Fcbs command is included in the configuration file (CONFIG.SYS) the resident size of DOS is increased.

## SPECIFYING THE LASTDRIVE

The final DOS 3.x network related command is Lastdrive.  It, like Fcbs, is executed via the Config.sys file.  Lastdrive is used to expand the number of drives that may be accessed by the system.  Without specifying Lastdrive a system may access drive A: through E:.

Throughout this text, we have referred to drives A:, B:, and C:.  These three drive designations usually refer to two floppy disk drives and a hard drive.  In unit 9 we discussed the addition of a RAM disk.  A system with two floppy drives and a hard disk would designate the RAM disk as drive D:.  The naming of additional drives continues up the alphabetic ladder.  Some systems may include all of the above plus a tape backup unit.  That unit might be referred to as the E: drive.

Unless specified otherwise, the PC system running under DOS 3.x assumes the last drive name available is E:. In other words, the Lastdrive command is automatically set to equal E, unless you indicate otherwise. PCs connected to a network may find this a limitation, so DOS provides the option of increasing the Lastdrive value.

It is not uncommon for networked PCs to have both **public** (shared) and **private** (limited access) drives or directories (also referred to as **volumes**). In fact, many networks divide a single hard disk into multiple directories, each designated as a different drive for a different user.

Let us examine two stations on a multi-station network.

---

**Station One**

Floppy drive = A:
Floppy drive = B:
Hard drive (public) = C:
RAM disk = D:
Tape backup unit = E:

**Station Two**

Floppy drive = A:
Floppy drive = B:
Hard disk (private) = C:
RAM disk = D:

---

The user on station two has access to six drives. When working on station two, the following drive designators could be used:

| A: drive | Floppy drive A: on Station Two |
| B: drive | Floppy drive B: on Station Two |
| C: drive | Hard disk (private) on Station Two |
| D: drive | RAM disk on Station Two Hard |
| E: drive | disk (public) on Station One Tape |
| F: drive | Backup Unit on Station One |

Notice that the drive designations are specific to each work station. Drive E: on station one is probably not going to be drive E: on any other workstation. Further, station two has drives designated beyond the default value of E:. In order for this configuration to work, the Lastdrive command must exist in the Config.sys file. Its form would be

LASTDRIVE = F

The syntax of the Lastdrive command is

LASTDRIVE = x

where x is equal to the last drive name.  The value must be alphabetic and the greatest value available would be Z.

There does not appear to be any gain or loss in memory or functionality by raising the Lastdrive value higher than necessary.  For instance, no damage results from making Lastdrive equal to Z, even if only the traditional A:, B:, and C: drives are physically present.

## NETWORK SOFTWARE COMMANDS

The software that is specific to each commercial network includes many additional commands.  Often, the network software includes modified versions of the DOS commands discussed throughout this text.  After you know DOS, learning network software is like relearning English with a slightly different accent.  The similarities far outweigh the differences.

The number of specific file-sharing commands in DOS is likely to increase in the near future.  Further, other standard DOS commands will probably be altered to accommodate additional multitasking and multiprocessing features.

## COMMAND REVIEW DICTIONARY

In this unit you have read about several DOS commands. Most commands have optional parameters. We have tried to cover both the common and the rarely used forms of each command. The following forms of this unit's commands are the most frequently used and should be reviewed carefully.

FCBS = 16,8                 Used within the Config.Sys file, this form of the command establishes a maximum of 16 files that may be open at one time. The command further indicates that the first 8 files loaded into memory have priority and will not be closed automatically in order to open a new file.

LASTDRIVE = F             Indicates the last drive name that can be legally accessed by DOS. Without using the Lastname command, the default is drive E:, i.e., only drives A:, B:, C:, D:, or E: may be accessed.

SHARE                      Loads support for file-sharing. This form uses the default settings.

## REVIEW QUESTIONS

1. What is the impetus behind the growth in local area networks?

2. Define local area network.

3. Why is file-sharing important?

4. List at least five topics to be considered before selecting or implementing a local area network.

5. What function does a network administrator perform?

6. What support for networks was added with DOS 3.x?

7. What function does the Share command serve?

8. What function does the Fcbs command serve?

9. What function does the Lastdrive command serve?

## DOCUMENTATION RESEARCH

In the IBM DISK OPERATING SYSTEM version 3.1 manual, read about the file control block and Lastdrive commands in chapter 4 before answering the following questions:

1. What is the maximum number of files open that may be specified in the Fcbs command?

2. What is the minimum number of open files that may be specified in the Fcbs command?

3. What is the range of values (minimum and maximum number of files specified by Fcbs) that may be opened and cannot be automatically closed by the operating system?

4. What purpose do file control blocks serve?

5. Is the Fcbs command effective when the computer system is not operating in a file-sharing (network) environment?

6. Is the Fcbs command executed from the keyboard? If so, when? If not, where is it used?

7. What happens if Lastdrive is set to less than the number of physical drives installed on your computer?

# UNIT

# 12

# DOS SHELLS

**SUPPLIES NEEDED**

The supplies that you will need for completing this unit are

1. IBM DISK OPERATING SYSTEM version 3.1 manual;
2. access to an IBM PC with hard-disk subsystem;
3. PC-DOS 3.1 installed on the hard-disk.

**OBJECTIVES**

After completing this unit,you will be able to

1. define the essential benefit offered by a DOS shell;
2. list and explain the four functional areas served by DOS shells;
3. discuss the concept of attribute setting and the related issue of file protection;
4. list and discuss three new commands provided as extended DOS features;
5. discuss key redefinition, macros, and keyboard enhancers as they relate to extended DOS features;
6. explain the concept of tagging and untagging and how it relates to manipulating multiple files.

225

## ASSIGNMENTS

Place a check in front of the assignments for this unit.

1. ____    Review and understand the following terms listed in the Computer Terms Dictionary (Appendix A): DOS shell, keyboard enhancer, macro, replaceable parameters.
2. ____    Guided Activity:  Creating a Simple DOS Shell.
3. ____    Review Questions.
4. ____    Documentation Research.


## WHAT IS A DOS SHELL--AND WHY DO I NEED ONE?

Microcomputer users are not uniform in their needs and levels of computing skills.  Secretaries, managers, engineers, and other end users are often not interested in learning a new software, such as DOS, just to enable them to complete their computing tasks.  To many, DOS is an inconvenience to be dealt with.  At the other end of the spectrum are users who can point out the gaps in IBM's operating system.  They will point to the lack of Move, Find a file, and Undelete commands.  In between are a host of people who loose files in subdirectories and find DOS's Backup and Restore commands tedious and slow.

A **DOS shell** is meant to address all these concerns by way of an interface of menus, new commands, and visual displays.  A DOS shell allows the user access to the power of DOS with less typing and less knowledge of PC-DOS or MS-DOS commands.


## EXPLORATION OF COMMERCIAL DOS SHELLS

All DOS shells are not created equally.  Four general functional areas are served by DOS shells, but not every shell addresses all four areas.  The four areas of user need are

1. menu generation;
2. file/disk backup utilities;
3. path utilities;
4. extended DOS features.

Some of the most popular application programs have been menu-driven.  You can scan a list of menu options and highlight or otherwise select one without typing more than one or two keystrokes.  Raw DOS does not provide that friendly interface.  Menu generators try to fill that need by providing a one- or two-keystroke access to application programs, such as word processor, spreadsheet, and data base programs.  You need not be concerned with where files are stored, in which subdirectory.  Menu generators often take a good deal of setup time.  The software must be configured to your exact system and subdirectory structure.  After the initial work is complete, the menu generated by the utility guides you through the maze with great ease.

File/disk backup utilities simply replace the DOS Backup and Restore commands.  Such utilities may be used to back up files to disk as DOS does, or they may be used in conjunction with tape backup systems.  Routinely, they include one feature which DOS does not--speed.  File/disk backup utilities run faster and more efficiently than the DOS commands.

The third category is the path utility. Visualizing paths, directories, and subdirectories on a DOS-formatted hard-disk can stretch the imagination. It can be especially confusing for the novice user or operator, who is more concerned with getting the job done than with understanding the intricacies of DOS. A path utility helps the user navigate through the maze of directories and subdirectories. The most common aspect of path utilities is a visual display of the directory tree with the current or default directory highlighted.

## EXTENDED DOS FEATURES

The fourth and final functional area is the addition of extended DOS features. In short, the DOS shell helps the user do things not available in DOS. The more noteworthy features include the addition of

* an attribute setting feature;
* file protection;
* a Find File command;
* key redefinition;
* macro creation;
* a Move command;
* a tag capability;
* an Undelete command.

In an earlier chapter, the Attrib command was discussed. It can be used to mark a file as read-only or read-and-write by altering one bit in the attribute byte. Four bits may be altered on the attribute byte under DOS 3.1 and higher. The four attributes mark the file as

1. archived;
2. a hidden file;
3. read-only;
4. a system file;

Some DOS shells allow the user to reset these attribute bits. For security purposes, marking a file as hidden may be helpful, since it will not be displayed when the Dir command is invoked. The archival bit may be altered to allow a file to be backed up, using the Backup command and the modified parameter, even if the file has not been changed since the last backup.

File protection includes the ability to assign a password to a file, directory, subdirectory, or disk. Some DOS shells go as far as providing the ability to encrypt data.

The DOS Find command will locate a specific phrase or text string in a specified file. However, it will not assist in finding that string in multiple files (without a lot of typing), nor will it help find a specific file buried within the maze on a hard-disk. The Find File command provided by some DOS shells meets this need.

Keyboard enhancers abound on the software shelves of retail outlets. They enable the user to redefine certain keys to perform nonstandard functions. A few of the DOS shells have picked up one aspect of the **keyboard enhancer** feature. They allow you to redefine the function keys. Within an application program, this can cause some problems, but operating at the DOS shell level, it can eliminate multiple keystrokes by the operator.

Macro creation is closely related. A **macro** is simply a collection of keystrokes. If your company has a long-winded name, a specified keyboard key can be defined to type out the entire name. Thus, one or two keystrokes becomes a macro capable of entering 20, 30, or more keystrokes.

DOS, in a clumsy sense, is capabile of moving a file from one location on a hard-disk to another. The process would include copying the file to its new location, comparing the two files to be sure the copy is identical, and then returning to the original file to erase it. One of the most common extended DOS features is the incorporation of a Move command. It allows the user to accomplish with one command what DOS would require three to do.

DOS allows commands to be executed on a related group of files only if their filenames are similar and the wildcard characters are used. For instance, the following group of text files could be erased using the command Del NEWSLTR?.TXT:

NEWSLTR1.TXT
NEWSLTR2.TXT
NEWSLTR3.TXT
NEWSLTR5.TXT
NEWSLTR7.TXT
NEWSLTR9.TXT

The tag capability of most DOS shells lets the user highlight multiple files and then execute one command on all the tagged or marked files. It is no longer necessary to try ingenious uses of the wildcard characters to delete or copy a group of files with dissimilar names. A complementary feature is the ability to untag files once marked and to undo a specific action just executed on a tagged group of files.

The Undelete command can be a lifesaver for operators who inadvertently wipe out a file of group of files. Its operation is based on the premise that the sectors and clusters used by the accidentally deleted file have not been subsequently reused by saving other files. Undelete is most successful if invoked immediately after the accidental erasure.

All four functions of the DOS shell fall under the general heading of file management utilities. The essential aim of any DOS shell is to make access and use of the operating system easier for the end user.

**GUIDED ACTIVITY:  CREATING A SIMPLE DOS SHELL**

In this Guided activity, you will create a rudimentary DOS shell.  As with any project, the initial work is to create a bare outline of the shell and then fill it out.  If you were designing this project from scratch, a great deal of planning would be required before you even touched the keyboard.  In this case, the authors have completed the desk work for you.

All previous exercises in this text have assumed a system with two floppy drives.  Because a DOS shell is most useful on a hard-disk computer system, this exercise assumes you are working on a computer with a hard-disk.  If your hard-disk is not drive C:, substitute the appropriate drive designator every time drive C: is mentioned.  Further, most files created in this activity should go into a subdirectory of the root directory.  In this exercise, that subdirectory is named "Batch."  You will also need access to the file called INPUTS, created in Unit 8.  You will copy it into the Batch subdirectory in this exercise.

SPECIAL NOTE:  This **is** a very long exercise.  Building even a simple DOS shell requires multiple files and numerous lines of code.  This exercise is intended to serve as a review of concepts and commands introduced in previous units.  Periodically during the exercise, we'll review information covered earlier in the text.  If you do not understand the use of certain commands and their parameters--use this activity as an opportunity to return to previous units and review.

SHORT CUT:  If you prefer to avoid the step-by-step process, refer to Appendix C.  It lists the exact lines for each file created.  Referring to Appendix C will also allow you to create the files with a word processor (which generates ASCII text files) and thus avoid using Edlin.  Just be sure to save each file as a text file and give it the filename specified in Appendix C.  If you choose this shortcut, be sure to first complete steps 1 through 10.  Then use your word processor to create all files in Appendix C.  When the files are complete, copy them into the Batch subdirectory created in step 4 and 5.  To finish the guided activity, complete steps 324-356.

1. Boot your computer system.

2. Enter date and time when prompted.

3. Be sure you are in the root directory and the DOS prompt appears as C>.

4. Type **MD BATCH**

5. Press <CR>.

6. Type **CD BATCH**

7. Press <CR>.

8. Insert your data diskette in drive A:.

9. Type **COPY A:INPUTS/V**

10. Press <CR>.

To begin the shell, you must create a main menu.  After defining choices at that level, you will proceed to flesh out the rest of the DOS shell.  In the following steps, you will create a main menu screen with three options and subsequently create a batch file to display the main menu screen.

11. Type **EDLIN MAINMENU.SCR**

12. Press <CR>.

13. Press <I>.

14. Press <CR>.

15. Press <CR> four times.

16. Press the <TAB> key three times.

17. Type **A SIMPLE DOS SHELL**

18. Press <CR> twice.

19. Press the <TAB> key twice.

20. Type **1.** and Press <TAB> once.

21. Type **Format a New Disk**

22. Press <CR> twice.

23. Press <TAB> twice.

24. Type **2.** and Press <TAB>.

25. Type **Backup Files**

26. Press <CR> twice.

27. Press <TAB> twice.

28. Type **3.** and Press <TAB> once.

29. Type **Exit to DOS**

30. Press <CR> twice.

31. Press <^C>.

32. Press <L> to list the file and Press <CR>.

Your monitor listing should appear as shown in Figure 12-1.

```
*L
    2:
    3:
    4:
    5:                     A SIMPLE DOS SHELL
    6:
    7:            1.    Format A New Disk
    8:
    9:            2.    Backup Files
   10:
   11:            3.    Exit To DOS
   12:
*_
```

FIGURE 12-1.  MAINMENU.SCR Listing

33. Press <E>.

34. Press <CR>.

The preceding steps simply created a menu screen.  In the following steps, you will create a short batch file to call or display MAINMENU.SCR.

35. Type **EDLIN MAINMENU.BAT**

36. Press <CR>.

37. Press <I> to insert text in this new batch file.

38. Press <CR>.

39. Type **ECHO OFF**

40. Press <CR>.

41. Type **CLS**

42. Press <CR>.

43. Type **TYPE MAINMENU.SCR**

44. Press <CR>.

45. Type **PROMPT ENTER CHOICE BY NUMBER $g**

46. Press <CR>.

47. Press ^C.

48. Press <L>.

49. Press <CR>.

The screen should appear as shown in Figure 12-2 below.

```
    *I
         1:*ECHO OFF
         2:*CLS
         3:*TYPE MAINMENU.SCR
         4:*PROMPT ENTER CHOICE BY NUMBER $g
         5:*^C

    *L
         1: ECHO OFF
         2: CLS
         3: TYPE MAINMENU.SCR
         4: PROMPT ENTER CHOICE BY NUMBER $g

    *_
```

FIGURE 12-2.  MAINMENU.BAT Listing

50. Press <E>.

51. Press <CR>.

The main menu includes three options.  Behind each must be a batch file to execute the desired action. Returning to DOS is the easiest option to program; that is where you will begin building.

52. Type **EDLIN 3.BAT**

53. Press <CR>.

54. Press <I>.

55. Press <CR>.

56. Type **ECHO OFF**

57. Press <CR>.

58. Type **PROMPT $p$g**

59. Press <CR>.

60. Type **CLS**

61. Press <CR>.

62. Press <^C>.

63. Press <L>.

64. Press <CR>.

Your monitor screen should include the text as shown in Figure 12-3 below.

```
  *I
        1:*ECHO OFF
        2:*PROMPT $p$g
        3:*CLS
        4:*^C
  *L
        1: ECHO OFF
        2: PROMPT $p$g
        3: CLS
  *_
```

FIGURE 12-3.  Listing of File 3.BAT

65. Press <E>.

66. Press <CR>.

Option one of the main menu must still be fleshed out.  In the following steps, you will create a batch file to invoke the Format command.  A few cautionary messages will also be included.

67. Type **EDLIN 1.BAT**

68. Press <CR>.

69. Press <I>.

70. Press <CR>.

71. Type **ECHO OFF**

72. Press <CR>.

73. Type **PROMPT $p$g**

74. Press <CR>.

75. Type **CLS**

76. Press <CR>.

77. Type **ECHO INSERT DISK TO BE FORMATTED IN DRIVE A:**

78. Press <CR>.

79. Type **ECHO ANY DATA ON THE DISK WILL BE DESTROYED!**

80. Press <CR>.

81. Type **PAUSE**

82. Press <CR>.

83. Type **ECHO ***

84. Press <CR>.

85. Type **ECHO * ***

86. Press <CR>.

87. Type **ECHO * * ***

88. Press <CR>.

89. Type **ECHO * * * * LAST CHANCE**

90. Press <CR>.

91. Type **ECHO * * * * TO SAVE ANY DATA ON DISK IN DRIVE A:**

92. Press <CR>.

93. Type **PAUSE**

94. Press <CR>.

95. Type **ECHO * * * * ***

96. Press <CR>.

97. Type **ECHO * * * * * ***

98. Press <CR>.

99. Type **ECHO * * * * * * ***

100. Press <CR>.

101. Type **ECHO * * * * * * * * TOO LATE!!**

102. Press <CR>.

103. Type **ECHO ***

104. Press <CR>.

105. Type **ECHO * ***

106. Press <CR>.

107. Type **ECHO * * ***

108. Press <CR>.

109. Type **ECHO * * * ***

110. Press <CR>.

111. Type **FORMAT A: <INPUTS**

112. Press <CR>.

113. Type **MAINMENU**

114. Press <CR>.

115. Press <^C>.

116. Type **1,22L**

117. Press <CR>.

The listing of the 1.BAT file is shown in Figure 12-4.

```
*1,22L
      1: echo off
      2: prompt $p$g
      3: cls
      4: echo INSERT DISK TO BE FORMATTED IN DRIVE A:
      5: echo ANY DATA ON THE DISK WILL BE DESTROYED!
      6: pause
      7: echo *
      8: echo * *
      9: echo * * *
     10: echo * * * * LAST CHANCE
     11: echo * * * * TO SAVE ANY DATA ON DISK IN DRIVE A:
     12: pause
     13: echo * * * *
     14: echo * * * * *
     15: echo * * * * * *
     16: echo * * * * * * * TOO LATE!!
     17: echo *
     18: echo * *
     19: echo * * *
     20: echo * * *
     21: FORMAT A: <INPUTS
     22: MAINMENU
*
```

FIGURE 12-4.  Listing of 1.BAT File

118. Press <E>.

119. Press <CR>.

Below the "Backup Files" option on the main menu, you will need to create a submenu of choices.  First you will create the screen file to be displayed, which will include the five options.  Next you will create another batch file called 2.BAT.  It will be invoked when option 2 is selected from the main menu.

120. Type **EDLIN BACKUP.SCR**

121. Press <CR>.

122. Press <I>.

123. Press <CR>.

124. Press <CR> four times.

125. Press <TAB> three times.

126. Type **BACKUP SUBMENU**

127. Press <CR> twice.

128. Press <TAB> twice.

129. Type **A.** and Press <TAB> once.

130. Type **Back up ALL files on Hard Disk**

131. Press <CR> twice.

132. Press <TAB> twice.

133. Type **B.** and Press <TAB> once.

134. Type **Back up ONLY Modified Hard Disk Files**

135. Press <CR> twice.

136. Press <TAB> twice.

137. Type **C.** and Press <TAB> once.

138. Type **Back up Files in a Subdirectory**

139. Press <CR> twice.

140. Press <TAB> twice.

141. Type **D.** and Press <TAB> once.

142. Type **Return to Main Menu**

143. Press <CR> twice.

144. Press <TAB> twice.

145. Type **E.** and Press <TAB> once.

146. Type **Exit to DOS**

147. Press <CR> three times.

148. Press <^C>.

149. Type **1,17L**

150. Press <CR>.

The listing for BACKUP.SCR should appear as shown in Figure 12-5 below.

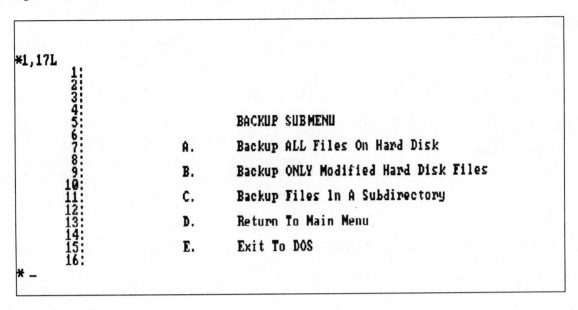

```
*1,17L
    1:
    2:
    3:
    4:
    5:            BACKUP SUBMENU
    6:
    7:     A.    Backup ALL Files On Hard Disk
    8:
    9:     B.    Backup ONLY Modified Hard Disk Files
   10:
   11:     C.    Backup Files In A Subdirectory
   12:
   13:     D.    Return To Main Menu
   14:
   15:     E.    Exit To DOS
   16:
*  _
```

FIGURE 12-5.  Listing Of Backup SubMenu Screen

151. Press <E>.

152. Press <CR>.

The next batch file will cause the backup menu (BACKUP.SCR file) to be displayed. This file is activated when you select option 2.  It is called 2.BAT.

153. Type **EDLIN 2.BAT**

154. Press <CR>.

155. Press <I>.

156. Press <CR>.

157. Type **ECHO OFF**

158. Press <CR>.

159. Type **PROMPT $p$g**

160. Press <CR>.

161. Type **CLS**

162. Press <CR>.

163. Type **TYPE BACKUP.SCR**

164. Press <CR>.

165. Type **PROMPT ENTER LETTER OF CHOICE $g**

166. Press <CR>.

167. Press <^C>.

168. Type **L**

169. Press <CR>.

The resulting screen display should appear as shown in Figure 12-6 below.

```
*I
    1:*ECHO OFF
    2:*PROMPT $p$g
    3:*CLS
    4:*TYPE BACKUP.SCR
    5:*PROMPT ENTER LETTER OF CHOICE $g
    6:*^C
*L
    1: ECHO OFF
    2: PROMPT $p$g
    3: CLS
    4: TYPE BACKUP.SCR
    5: PROMPT ENTER LETTER OF CHOICE $g

*_
```

FIGURE 12-6.  Listing for File Named 2.BAT

170. Press <E>.

171. Press <CR>.

Once the submenu screen is invoked, additional batch files are needed behind it.  By creating batch files named A.BAT, B.BAT, C.BAT, D.BAT, and E.BAT, you enable the user to select an option by using two keystrokes--the letter of their option plus a <CR>.

The first option is A, which invokes the Backup command and performs a complete hard-disk backup.

172. Type **EDLIN A.BAT**

173. Press <CR>.

174. Type <I> to insert text in this new batch file.

175. Press <CR>.

176. Type **ECHO OFF**

177. Press <CR>.

178. Type **PROMPT $p$g**

179. Press <CR>.

180. Type **CLS**

181. Press <CR>.

182. Type **TYPE BACKUP.MSG**

183. Press <CR>.

184. Type **PAUSE**

185. Press <CR>.

186. Type **CLS**

187. Press <CR>.

188. Type **BACKUP C:\ A:/S**

189. Press <CR>.

190. Type **PAUSE**

191. Press <CR>.

192. Type **MAINMENU**

193. Press <CR>.

194. Press <^C>.

195. Press <L>.

196. Press <CR>.

The screen should appear as shown in Figure 12-7 below.

```
*L
      1:  ECHO OFF
      2:  PROMPT $p$g
      3:  CLS
      4:  TYPE BACKUP.MSG
      5:  PAUSE
      6:  CLS
      7:  BACKUP C:\ A:/S
      8:  PAUSE
      9:  MAINMENU
*_
```

FIGURE 12-7.  Listing Of A.BAT File

197. Press <E>.

198. Press <CR>.

Since the difference between options A and B is a switch on the Backup command, you can take a shortcut and simply make a duplicate of the A.BAT file, name it B.BAT, and then edit the file with Edlin.

199. Type **COPY A.BAT B.BAT**

200. Press <CR>.

201. Type **EDLIN B.BAT**

202. Press <CR>.

The monitor screen will respond with the message

> End of input file
> *
> ‾

203. Press <L>.

204. Press <CR>.

The screen should display the same file listing as generated by A.BAT in Figure 12-7. The only difference between the two files is in line 7.

205. Press <7>.

206. Press <CR>.

207. Press <F2> followed by <S>.

208. Type **S/M**

209. Press <CR>.

Your screen will appear as shown in Figure 12-8 below.

```
*L
       1:*ECHO OFF
       2: PROMPT $p$g
       3: CLS
       4: TYPE BACKUP.MSG
       5: PAUSE
       6: CLS
       7: BACKUP C:\ A:/S
       8: PAUSE
       9: MAINMENU
*7
       7:*BACKUP C:\ A:/S
       7:*BACKUP C:\ A:/S/M
*_
```

FIGURE 12-8.  Screen Listing When Editing B.BAT File

210. Press <E>.

211. Press <CR>.

In the two files A.BAT and B.BAT, you referenced another file named BACKUP.MSG.  The next few steps will create that file.

212. Type **EDLIN BACKUP.MSG**

213. Press <CR>.

214. Press <I>.

215. Press <CR>.

216. Press <CR> four times.

217. Press <TAB> three times.

218. Type **All files will be backed up to drive A:.**

219. Press <CR> twice.

220. Press <TAB> three times.

221. Type **Be sure you have a sufficient number of**

222. Press <CR>.

223. Press <TAB> three times.

224. Type **blank formatted diskettes.  It can take**

225. Press <CR>.

226. Press <TAB> three times.

227. Type **25 diskettes to back up 10 megabytes of data.**

228. Press <CR> three times.

229. Press <^C>.

Your screen should appear as shown in Figure 12-9.

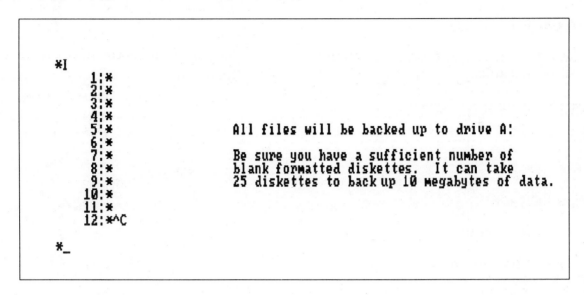

```
*I
      1:*
      2:*
      3:*
      4:*
      5:*          All files will be backed up to drive A:
      6:*
      7:*          Be sure you have a sufficient number of
      8:*          blank formatted diskettes.  It can take
      9:*          25 diskettes to back up 10 megabytes of data.
     10:*
     11:*
     12:*^C

   *_
```

FIGURE 12-9.  Listing Of BACKUP.MSG File

230. Press <E>.

231. Press <CR>.

A couple of little batch files are needed to cover menu options D and E.  The E option returns control to DOS, i.e., exits to DOS, so an identical file to 3.BAT may be used.  The shortest method is to copy 3.BAT, making a new file E.BAT.

232. Type **COPY 3.BAT E.BAT**

233. Press <CR>.

Option D simply switches control back to the main menu.  That can be accomplished with a single-line batch file called D.BAT.

234. Type **EDLIN D.BAT**

235. Press <CR>.

236. Press <I>.

237. Press <CR>.

238. Type **MAINMENU**

239. Press <CR>.

240. Press <^C>.

241. Press <E>.

242. Press <CR>.

You are down to one more menu option to be defined. It is option C, which backs up a specific subdirectory of files.

To accomplish this final task, you will need to create three files. The first is very similar to A.BAT and B.BAT. It is so similar that you can once again use the Copy command, then modify the new file slightly with Edlin. The second file is a screen file and the third is a special batch file, which invokes the Backup command using a **replaceable parameter**.

243. Type **COPY A.BAT C.BAT**

244. Press <CR>.

245. Type **EDLIN C.BAT**

246. Press <CR>.

247. Press <L>.

248. Press <CR>.

The screen display should appear as shown in Figure 12-10.

```
*L
        1: ECHO OFF
        2: PROMPT $p$g
        3: CLS
        4: TYPE BACKUP.MSG
        5: PAUSE
        6: CLS
        7: BACKUP C:\ A:/S
        8: PAUSE
        9: MAINMENU
*_
```

FIGURE 12-10.  Listing Of C.BAT File

249. Press <7>.

250. Press <CR>.

251. Type **TYPE BKUPSUB.SCR** and Press <CR>.

252. Type **8,9D**

253. Press <CR>.

254. Press <I>.

255. Press <CR>.

256. Type **PROMPT TYPE "ONLY" AND SUBDIRECTORY NAME...PRESS RETURN $g**

257. Press <CR>.

258. Press <^C>.

259. Press <L>.

260. Press <CR>.

The screen should display the lines shown in Figure 12-11.

```
*L
     1: ECHO OFF
     2: PROMPT $p$g
     3: CLS
     4: TYPE BACKUP.MSG
     5: PAUSE
     6: CLS
     7: TYPE BKUPSUB.SCR
     8: PROMPT TYPE "ONLY" AND SUBDIRECTORY NAME...PRESS RETURN $g

*_
```

FIGURE 12-11.  Listing Of Edited C.BAT File

261. Press <E>.

262. Press <CR>.

The next file simply provides text directions for the operator.

263. Type **EDLIN BKUPSUB.SCR**

264. Press <CR>.

265. Press <I>.

266. Press <CR>.

267. Press <CR> four times.

268. Press <TAB> twice.

269. Type **This menu option will allow you to make a**

270. Press <CR>.

271. Press <TAB> twice.

272. Type **complete backup of any ONE subdirectory.**

273. Press <CR> twice.

274. Press TAB twice.

275. Type **In order to begin the backup operation,**

276. Press <CR>.

277. Press TAB twice.

278. Type **simply type the subdirectory name preceded**

279. Press <CR>.

280. Press TAB twice.

281. Type **by the word ONLY (for example: ONLY DOS).**

282. Press <CR> twice.

283. Press <TAB> twice.

284. Type **This option will only work for subdirectories**

285. Press <CR>.

286. Press <TAB> twice.

287. Type **immediately under the Root directory.**

288. Press <CR>.

289. Press <^C>.

290. Press <L>.

291. Press <CR>.

The monitor screen should display the text lines as shown in Figure 12-12.

```
*1
        3:
        4:
        5:                    This menu option will allow you to make a
        6:                    complete backup of any ONE subdirectory.
        7:
        8:                    In order to begin the backup operation,
        9:                    simply type the subdirectory name preceded
       10:                    by the word ONLY (for example: ONLY DOS).
       11:
       12:                    This option will only work for subdirectories
       13:                    immediately under the Root directory.
*  _
```

FIGURE 12-12.  BKUPSUB.SCR File Listing

292. Press <E>.

293. Press <CR>.

The final batch file needed to complete this simple DOS shell is called ONLY.BAT.  The next few steps will complete the exercise except for final testing.

## REPLACEABLE PARAMETERS

Before proceeding, a brief discussion of replaceable parameters is needed.  DOS has ten such parameters, each numbered 0 to 9 and preceded by a percentage sign (%0, %1, %2, %3, %4, %5, %6, %7, %8, %9).  They may be inserted into a batch file to represent a parameter or switch.  For instance, if you created a batch file called ARCHIVE.BAT, its text might resemble the following:

    COPY  C:*.DOC  A:/V

By typing ARCHIVE, all document files, those with the .DOC extension, would be duplicated on the disk in the A: drive.  Suppose you wanted to back up all worksheets with the Copy command. ARCHIVE.BAT would not work--unless you used a replaceable parameter.

The file could be rewritten

    COPY  C:*.%1  A:/V

By typing the following commands at the keyboard, different results are generated:

    ARCHIVE DOC Duplicates all files with the .DOC extension.
    ARCHIVE TXT Duplicates all files with the .TXT extension.
    ARCHIVE WK Duplicates all files with the .WK extension.
    ARCHIVE COM Duplicates all files with the .COM extension.

It should be noted that the %0 replaceable parameter is restricted in use. It can substitute only for the name of the batch file. All other replaceable parameters are less restricted in use. All ten replaceable parameters may be used with one command if needed.

**GUIDED ACTIVITY:  CREATING A SIMPLE DOS SHELL (continued)**

305. Type **EDLIN ONLY.BAT**

306. Press <CR>.

307. Press <I>.

308. Press <CR>.

309. Type **ECHO OFF**

310. Press <CR>.

311. Type **BACKUP C:\%1 A:/S**

312. Press <CR>.

313. Type **PROMPT $p$g**

314. Press <CR>.

315. Type **PAUSE**

316. Press <CR>.

317. Type **MAINMENU**

318. Press <CR>.

319. Press <^C>.

320. Press <L>.

321. Press <CR>.

The monitor will display the lines shown in Figure 12-13.

```
*L
      1: ECHO OFF
      2: BACKUP C:\%1 A:/S
      3: PROMPT $p$g
      4: PAUSE
      5: MAINMENU

*_
```

FIGURE 12-13.  Listing Of ONLY.BAT File

322. Press <E>.

323. Press <CR>.

After all those lines of code, you have created a shell capable of three or four functions.  The work is done up front in order to make day-to-day operations easier for novice and intermediate computer users.  The system is still untested.  However, if you carefully double-checked your code each step of the way, the system will work.

324. Type **MAINMENU**

325. Press <CR>.

The monitor screen will display the main menu you created earlier.  Test each option on each menu.  If you need to break out of a loop or any portion of the shell, Press <CTRL BREAK>.

After testing each option, go back, using Edlin to correct any errors.  Then proceed to the next few steps.  They will allow you to create an AUTOEXEC.BAT file that automatically loads your DOS shell program.

326. Press <3>.

327. Press <CR>.

328. Type **CD\** and Press <CR> to return to the root directory.

329. Type **DIR AUTOEXEC.\*** and Press <CR> to see if an AUTOEXEC.BAT file exists.

If you find an AUTOEXEC.BAT file, rename it so the contents are not lost. This is accomplished in the next two steps. If no file is found, skip the next two steps.

330. Type **REN AUTOEXEC.BAT AUTOEXEC.OLD**

331. Press <CR>.

332. Type **EDLIN AUTOEXEC.BAT**

333. Press <CR>.

If you do not get the "New File" message from Edlin, then the renaming of the old AUTOEXEC.BAT file was not successful. In that case, you must press <Q> followed by the <CR>. Then press <Y>.

334. Press <I>.

335. Press <CR>.

336. Type **PATH C:\;C:\DOS;A:\** (This step assumes your DOS files are in a "\DOS" subdirectory. Further, there should be a space after the "H" in PATH but no other spaces in the command line.)

337. Press <CR>.

338. Type **PROMPT $p$g**

339. Press <CR>.

340. Type **CD BATCH**

341. Press <CR>.

342. Type **MAINMENU**

343. Press <CR>.

344. Press <^C>.

345. Press <L>.

346. Press <CR>.

The new AUTOEXEC.BAT file should include the lines of text as shown in Figure 12-14.

```
*L
    1:  PATH C:\;C:\DOS;A:\
    2:  PROMPT $p$g
    3:  CD BATCH
    4:  MAINMENU

*_
```

FIGURE 12-14.  Listing Of AUTOEXEC.BAT File

347. Press <E>.

348. Press <CR>.

349. Press **CTRL**, **ALT** and **DEL** simultaneously to reboot your system.

When the AUTOEXEC.BAT file is executed, you should find yourself facing the main menu you created.

Experiment again with your DOS shell.  Try each option to make sure it is functional.  Can you think of better ways to accomplish the same DOS shell tasks?

What additional features would you include in your DOS shell?  Some easy extensions of the shell might include features to

 1. format bootable diskettes;
 2. load your word processor;
 3. load your spreadsheet program;
 4. load a data base management program;
 5. load a communications program;
 6. move a file from one directory to another;
 7. perform a disk copy;
 8. perform a disk compare.

When you are completely done with the DOS shell, and have experimented with it, complete the following steps:

350. Exit from the DOS shell at the main menu by pressing <3> and then Press <CR>.

351. Type **CD\**

352. Press <CR>.

353. Type **DEL AUTOEXEC.BAT**

354. Press <CR>.

If you had to rename an existing AUTOEXEC.BAT file earlier, then proceed with the next two steps. Otherwise, you have completed this guided activity.

355. Type **REN AUTOEXEC.OLD AUTOEXEC.BAT**

356. Press <CR>.

## REVIEW QUESTIONS

1. Why is a DOS shell helpful to users with varying skill levels?

2. What are the four functional areas served by DOS shells?

3. Why is a menu generator a boon to end users?

4. What is the most common feature of a path utility?

5. List eight extended DOS features.  Describe what each does.

6. What do the attribute setting feature and file protection have to do with security of files and data?

7. Define a keyboard macro.

8. How are keyboard enhancers, macros, and DOS shells related?

9. What is the benefit of a tag feature in a DOS shell?

10. Why might an Undelete command be ineffective?

## DOCUMENTATION RESEARCH

Read section 7 of the IBM DISK OPERATING SYSTEM version 3.1 manual.

1. Review the commands listed in section 7 of the DOS manual.  If you were designing a DOS shell, what additional commands would you include?

UNIT

# 13

# THE FUTURE OF
# IBM PC-DOS

**SUPPLIES NEEDED**

No supplies are needed to complete this unit.

**OBJECTIVES**

After completing this unit, you will be able to

1. define the five user concerns for the future of DOS;
2. define multitasking;
3. define multiprocessing;
4. define upward compatibility;
5. explain the difference between expanded and extended memory.

## ASSIGNMENTS

Place a check in front of the assignments for this unit.

1. ____ Review and understand the following terms listed in the Computer Terms Dictionary (Appendix A): bank switching, central processing unit, emulation, expanded memory, extended memory, interface, kernel, megabyte, multiprocessing, multitasking, upward compatibility, and user-friendly.
2. ____ Review Questions.
3. ____ Documentation Research.


## WHAT'S THE NEXT VERSION OF DOS?

In May of 1986, IBM began conducting seminars outlining the technical specifications of a new version of DOS. DOS 3.2 had been released and the media was calling the new operating system DOS 5.0. The seminars were held for software developers in order to give them a head start in developing or modifying their applications to run under the new DOS.

Although IBM refused to comment on the new DOS, several trade publications reported the specifics of the briefing. The details seem to indicate that IBM and Microsoft are listening to users on at least three of five concerns. Before we examine those concerns individually, let's find out what happened to DOS versions between 3.2 and 5.0.

In late 1986, Microsoft was still working on an unreleased version of the operating system, referred to as DOS 4.0, but IBM had already indicated that it would bypass that version. It would neither market nor put its stamp of approval on DOS 4.0.

To understand this development requires a brief history of the **central processing unit** (CPU) of the IBM family of personal computers. The Original IBM PC and XT used the Intel Corporation 8088 microprocessor. Compatible manufacturers seized on the Intel 8086, processor which executes the same instructions and programs as the 8088, but is faster. The 8086 employs a 16-bit external data path rather than the 8-bit path of the 8088. When the IBM PC AT was introduced, it used a new Intel 80286 chip. The latter is a far more powerful microprocessor, also designed to handle **multitasking**.

Microsoft's version 4.0 is intended to provide multitasking capabilities with the Intel 8088 and 8086 chip. Rather than endorse a software solution to multitasking, on a microprocessor not originally designed for that purpose, IBM chose to proceed with a combined software (unofficially called DOS 5.0) and hardware (Intel 80286 chip) solution. One further unofficial version of DOS is in the works. DOS 6.0 is supposedly planned to provide **multiprocessing** capabilities on the even more powerful Intel 80386 microprocessor.

Despite all the unofficial leaks on future versions of DOS, it is clear that IBM will not be bound by someone else's rumors. In late October 1986 came word that IBM will not call the new version DOS 5.0, but will instead label it Advanced DOS 1.0.

## FIVE USER CONCERNS FOR FUTURE DOS DIRECTIONS

Five areas of concern around which discussion of future DOS versions has centered are as follows:

1. expanded memory;
2. multitasking capabilities;
3. multiprocessing capabilities;
4. upward compatibility;
5. user-friendliness.


## EXPANDED MEMORY

The first area of concern can be illustrated by the following anecdote. Suppose that a manager has an IBM PC on his desk. The machine is linked to a Burroughs B5900 mainframe computer using an InterCom 1000 **emulation** board produced by MidWest Data Systems. The card uses DataComm software to emulate the Burroughs, i.e., make the desktop computer look and act like a mainframe terminal. The same computer has a Juniper II card, produced by Rohm Corporation, which gives the computer access to a modem pool for telecommunications. The Juniper II software stays resident in memory at all times. This manager uses the Smart Software System produced by Innovative Software Inc. Further, several memory-resident programs are used, including a keyboard enhancer, notepad/calendar, and public domain screen-saver utility. One day the manager goes to spell-check a document and gets the following message: "insufficient memory to load spellchecker."

The Intel 8088 microprocessor can address only one **megabyte** (1024K) of memory at one time. DOS must reserve some of that memory for special functions. The requirements of DOS 3.2 (and earlier) coupled with the microprocessor's limitations leave only 640K available for loaded portions of DOS, application programs, data, and memory-resident programs. In the anecdote about the manager, all available memory was used up. No memory space remained into which the spellchecker program could be loaded.

At top of the list for most experienced or power users is the need for DOS to access more memory. As application programs expand capabilities, they take more memory. As the user **interface** becomes more friendly and graphic, it takes more memory. As users add more memory-resident functions (address books, auto-dialers, notepads, calendars, electronic mail, spelling checkers, thesauruses, DOS shells, clock software, etc.), more memory is consumed.

The new generation of 80286 machines can address up to 16 megabytes of internal memory (RAM) running in protected mode. For the older machines using the 8088 microprocessor, the alternative is a **bank switching** scheme used by **expanded memory** boards on the market. Any long term, viable solution must include a revision of DOS.


## ADDITIONAL NOTES ON MEMORY

Most users refer to their personal computers as 256K, 512K, or 640K machines. The reference is really to the amount of RAM installed in the PC. You may have read that the current versions of DOS only allow the operating system to address 640K at one time. The technically accurate limit for an 8088 or 8086 microprocessor operating under DOS 3.x (or lower) is one megabyte of addressable memory. That megabyte is broken into sixteen different 64K memory blocks. Figure 13-1 illustrates the different blocks of memory and their function.

Note that block 0 through 9 compose the standard 640K of RAM which is ordinary user memory. Part of this 640K is consumed by DOS, BASIC (if loaded), application programs, memory resident software, and data entered by the user. Blocks 10 through 15 include RAM dedicated to specific functions (work space for the standard and extended video display) and ROM, i.e., IBM BASIC stored in ROM is part of the one megabyte.

The clear advantage of the new 80286 and 80386 machines is the ability to address up to 16 megabytes of memory (both RAM and ROM) instead of just one megabyte.

| Memory Block Number | Memory Range | Uses of Memory |
|---|---|---|
| 0 | 0-64K | Includes DOS and BASIC work area (when loaded), and keyboard buffer. DOS 3.x consumes about 36-40K of this area. |
| 1 | 64-128K | User work area. |
| 2 | 128-192K | User work area. |
| 3 | 192-256K | User work area. |
| 4 | 256-320K | User work area. |
| 5 | 320-384K | User work area. |
| 6 | 384-448K | User work area. |
| 7 | 448-512K | User work area. |
| 8 | 512-576K | User work area. |
| 9 | 576-640K | User work area. |
| 10 | 640-704K | Extended memory for video display. |
| 11 | 704-768K | Standard memory for video display. |
| 12 | 768-832K | XT hard disk and EGA board ROM expansion.* |
| 13 | 832-896K | Cartridge memory on PCjr. |
| 14 | 896-960K | Cartridge memory on PCjr. |
| 15 | 960-1024K | System ROM-BIOS, POST, and ROM-BASIC area. |

FIGURE 13-1. Sixteen Blocks of PC Memory and Related Functions.

* This memory typically resides on the hard disk controller card or the Enhanced Graphics Adapter (EGA) board.

## MULTITASKING

Most experienced computer users still remember the initial glow of computing, when accomplishing anything on the machine is exciting. After the initial euphoria, the personal computer steadily becomes a valuable tool, but still just a tool. When that stage is reached, the manager, secretary, or clerk seeks to accomplish tasks better and faster rather than simply computerizing for the sake of computerizing. Once the tool is integral to the flow of business, the major concern becomes completing tasks faster. Time spent waiting for the computer to complete a task is unproductive time. Unless you can scurry around doing other non-computing tasks, waiting for a large spreadsheet to recalculate or waiting for the printer to complete a long document--is a bore.

Multitasking is the capability of a microprocessor to handle several tasks at one time. Some software solutions have been created, such as internal print buffers, but the personal computer is still basically a single-task machine. The 8088 machines may be pretty much at the mercy of whatever Microsoft's DOS 4.0 provides in this area, but the newer 80286 machines have the hardware, the microprocessor, to tackle multitasking. Now the wait is for an enhanced version of DOS.

## MULTIPROCESSING

Concurrent with the need to do more tasks at the same time, many enterprises are discovering the need to handle multiple users at one time on a single machine. The rumored DOS 6.0 will tackle this problem by allowing the concurrent execution of multiple DOS work sessions on a single Intel 80386 CPU. This enhancement will be a boon to both networked machines and multiuser configurations.

Non-IBM software and hardware is already available to create a multiuser machine out of a standard IBM PC or XT. Special interface cards are placed in the personal computer which link it to additional slave stations. With non-IBM vendor software, the system can support one user per slave station, with each user sharing the CPU, memory, disk drives, and other peripherals. A small department that needs only two or three work stations may find this type of configuration far more cost-effective than buying multiple personal computers and networking them together. But there are drawbacks to this type of multiuser system.

1. Often runs slower than non-multiuser systems.
2. Typically only two additional work stations may be linked to one PC. Beyond that, the system must be networked.
3. Uses a special system software which may conflict with other software in use.
4. Application software on the system may react unpredictably unless it is a network version or the multiuser software allows a user to lock others out of a file while in-use.
5. Depending on the future direction of DOS, this may become obsolete equipment, unless the manufacturer is committed to continual enhancements and upgrades.

Ultimately, the solution for multiprocessing rests in the hands of the operating system developers. The microcomputer is no longer just a one-person machine. The expectation is that future versions of DOS will add to and enhance the networking and multiuser capabilities of the personal computer.

## UPWARD COMPATIBILITY

People and enterprises do not like to make a habit of purchasing expensive equipment that will shortly be obsolete. IBM pioneered the concept of families of computers allowing users to upgrade to bigger, more powerful machines. Coupled with that concept is the assurance that new developments, both in software and hardware, will provide a migration path for users. No one should wake up to find their machine unsupported and unloved. Providing the capapbility to upgrade machines and avoid planned obsolesence is the essence of **upward compatability**.

To date, every new version of DOS has supported all machines in the IBM personal computer family. Everyone hopes that is a tradition for the future.

The unannounced Advanced DOS 1.0 (or DOS 5.0) is expected to add numerous capabilities, but users and developers hope it will also run old applications. The documents released in IBM's May 1986 technical briefings indicate that PC-DOS 3.0, 3.1, and 3.2 applications will run without modification in the lower 640K of memory. Remember, the 80286 can address 16 megabytes of memory compared to the 640K of the 8088 processor. The ability to run these older applications is incorporated into the upcoming DOS via a "DOS 3.x compatibility box."

## USER-FRIENDLINESS

Operating systems, almost by definition, have traditionally not been creatures for the novice user to grasp. Even students of the operating system find strange conventions, unusual syntax, and user-unfriendly interfaces. PC-DOS and MS-DOS have no help screens, and sometimes use syntax that can befuddle an English major.

The intermediate solution is to acquire a DOS shell to make DOS less cryptic and more friendly. The long-range solution rests with software developers, specifically that team of men and women at Microsoft who create the operating system. The trend may be toward the use of graphic interfaces, such as used by Apple's Macintosh. IBM has developed TopView, and Microsoft has its own graphic interface called Windows. A future version of DOS may incorporate these types of **user-friendly** interfaces into the operating system software. Before such a development becomes reality, several hurdles must be overcome. Graphic interfaces require lots of memory, a graphic display and adapter, and a fixed disk. Hardware requirements often slow down the development of new software.

## ADVANCED DOS 1.0, OR PC-DOS 5.0?

Whatever the name of the new DOS expected in the first quarter of 1987, IBM and Microsoft appear to be addressing the need for upward compatibility, multitasking capabilities, and more memory. Multiprocessing will probably wait for a future version, and user-friendliness will clearly be in the eyes of the beholder. No one can know if DOS will become friendlier until it is in general release. There is some indication that the new DOS will incorporate the **kernel** portion of the Microsoft Windows environment. The kernel is the portion of Windows which includes operating-system-like code such as multitasking and memory management programming. That would be a step in the right direction.

Some of the anticipated features will only help users of the 80286 machines, such as the IBM PC AT and compatibles. Examples would be the ability to address up to 16 megabytes of RAM, and true multitasking.

In the long run, DOS must change and improve.  New hardware and software advances dictate that the operating system must be growing and vital.  Users who once were enamored with 640K (after starting with 64K machines), now think in terms of megabytes.  Managers who once were satisfied with unfriendly prompts now want graphic interfaces.  Users are never satisfied, and shouldn't be, with yesterday's breakthroughs and enhancements.

**ADDITIONAL REFERENCES ON DEVELOPMENTS IN PC-DOS AND MS-DOS**

The history of PC-DOS and MS-DOS is written daily.  It could be a full time career keeping pace with new developments, enhancements, bugs and rumors.  The following publications are helpful in providing periodic updates on DOS.

INFOWORLD, P.O. Box 1018, Southeastern, PA 19398, published weekly.
PC MAGAZINE, P.O. Box 2443, Boulder, CO 80321, published bi-weekly.
PC WEEK, One Park Avenue, 4th Floor, New York, NY 10016, published weekly.
PC WORLD, P.O. Box 6700, Bergenfield, NJ 07621, published monthly.
PERSONAL COMPUTING, P.O. Box 2941, Boulder, CO 80321, published monthly.

**REVIEW QUESTIONS**

1. Why is IBM not endorsing DOS version 4.0, and how is that decision linked to the Intel 8088 microprocessor?

2. What is the difference between multitasking and multiprocessing?

3. What is the difference between expanded and extended memory?  Which is better?

4. What is the driving force behind the need for multitasking?

5. What are the disadvantages of the current non-IBM multiuser configurations?

6. Define upward compatibility.  Who developed the concept?  Why is it important to hardware and software purchasers?

7. What solutions to the lack of user-friendliness exist with current versions of DOS?

## DOCUMENTATION RESEARCH

Because the IBM DISK OPERATING SYSTEM Version 3.1 manual does not address the issue of enhancements to future versions of DOS, Document Research for this chapter requires access to trade publications such as PC WEEK, INFOWORLD, PC MAGAZINE, PERSONAL COMPUTING, or similar publications.

1. Research and expand on one of the five areas of user concern for future versions of DOS.

2. Research and compare Microsoft's Windows and IBM's TopView.

3. Research and discuss the difference between Intel's 8088, 8086, 80286, and 80386 microprocessor chips. How do the differences affect the end user?

# COMPUTER TERMS DICTIONARY

The terms contained in this dictionary are used throughout the text. Be sure to reference this section if a term is not defined within the text.

**Alternative processing strategies**    One facet of a disaster recovery plan that deals with finding other sites or machines for data processing in an emergency situation.

**Archive**    To back up or make a duplicate copy.

**Asynchronous port**    A serial port. See Serial port.

**Attrib**    The DOS command that toggles a file between a read-only state and a read-and-write state.

**Attribute byte**    The eleventh byte of a directory listing which includes the read-only bit set by Attrib.

**Background task**    In a multitasking environment, the task with lower priority is referred to as the background task. When competition arises between the foreground and background tasks over access to the CPU, the higher-priority task wins. Foreground tasks always win over background tasks.

**Backup**    The DOS command that creates a mirror image of a file for archival purposes.

**Backup disks**

Diskettes on which files created by the Backup command are placed.

**Bank switching**

A scheme used by expanded memory boards. In this strategy, the microprocessor cannot address more than 1 megabyte (640K of usable RAM) at a time. The expanded memory is treated in a fashion similar to storing data on a disk. The most frequently accessed memory is stored in the lower 640K.

**BASIC**

Beginner's All-purpose Symbolic Instruction Code. A computer language developed at Dartmouth College to be used by students studying computer science.

**Basic Input/Output System**

BIOS is the portion of the disk operating system which is hardware dependent. It provides an interface between the operating system and the specific hardware used (i.e. microprocessor) and peripherals (i.e. hard disk, disk drives, monitor, etc).

**Baud rate**

The rate at which data is communicated to a peripheral device or to another computer. Baud equates with bits per second. Common rates for telecommunication include 300, 1200, and 2400 baud. Mainframes often communicate with their terminals at rates of 9600 baud or greater.

**Bit**

The smallest unit of storage or memory, represented either by the absence (0) or presence (1) of electrical current. Eight bits equal one byte, and one byte typically represents one character such as a number or letter.

**Boilerplate documents**

Standard blocks of text that are reused in numerous documents with only slight modification. A time-saving strategy.

**Boot**

The process of turning on a computer, which in turn loads the operating system and other software into RAM.

**Byte**

A unit of storage (memory) composed of eight bits. One byte can represent one character such as a letter or number.

**Cabling**

Refers to the type of connections used between work stations on a network. Types of cabling include twisted pair, coaxial, etc.

**Central processing unit**

See CPU.

**Compatibles**

Often referred to as IBM clones or compatibles. These microcomputers are produced by non-IBM manufacturers who strive to make their machines run software exactly as a true IBM computer would. Compatibles often improve upon the basic IBM machine, i.e. faster clock speed, additional slots, while still striving for software compatibility.

**Complete filename**

Includes the drive designator, file specification, and file extension.

**Config.sys**

Configuration file used with DOS; must be contained in the root directory, and includes several DOS commands, among them the Fcbs command.

**Copy-protection**

A strategy by which the ability to duplicate software is restricted.

**CPU**

The central processing unit (i.e., the 8088, 80286, or 80386 microprocessor or part of a computer that manipulates data and text.

**Databits**

Another term for word size. Indicates if a word (character transmitted) is 7 or 8 bits long.

**Disaster recovery plan**

A comprehensive plan to anticipate an emergency that will interfere with normal computing, and to propose alternatives. The basic component of every plan is periodic, complete system backups.

**Disk server**

A hard-disk on one work station in a network, which is used by all work stations for storing files.

**Display adapter**

A card or board in the microcomputer that contains the circuitry to drive a monitor. Display adapters come in several varieties, including monochrome, color, graphics, and enhanced graphics. A monochrone adapter is required to drive a monochrome monitor. Likewise, a color display adapter is required to run a color monitor.

**DOS**

The disk operating system is composed of coded instructions that tell the computer how to behave like a computer. These instructions cover management of internal communications, error checking, memory usage, data storage, data retrieval, data deletion, and device configuration.

**DOS command**

A word or phrase that executes a machine language routine stored either in ROM, on disk, or in memory.

**DOS prompt**

Typically the greater-than sign ( > ), preceded by a letter that designates the default drive.

**DOS shell**

A software program that enhances DOS by adding additional functions such as a menu generator, path utility, file/disk backup utility, and extended DOS features.

**Drive designation**

Indicates the drive on which a file is located.

**Emulation**

The process whereby one work station looks and behaves like another; i.e., an IBM PC can emulate a Burroughs B5900, IBM 4381 or other mainframe computer.

**End-of-File Mark**

A character in an ASCII text file generated by pressing the F6 key or CTRL-Z. This special character marks the end of the file on disk.

**Enterprise**

Any operation about which data is generated and stored on a computer system. An enterprise may be a person, department, company, state, institution, or similar entity.

**Expanded memory**

A system of using more than 1 megabyte (or 640K of usable) RAM by bank switching. The CPU still cannot access more than 640K, but the expanded memory amount is available in RAM rather than on disk. Disk access is always slower than expanded memory access.

**Extended memory**

Available in machines using the Intel 80286 microchip, which can address memory above the 1-megabyte barrier imposed by older Intel 8088 or 8086 machines. The amount of memory that may be simultaneously addressed is "extended" to 16 megabytes.

**Extension**

A portion of the complete filename that follows the file specification and a delimiter. Can be up to three characters long.

**External commands**

DOS commands that must be loaded from disk each time they are executed.

**FAT**

The file allocation table stores information that indicates the sectors assigned to each file on a diskette or hard disk. FAT also indicates the sectors on a disk which are free and may be used to store new data or new files.

**File control block**

Stores data relative to a specific file used in a computing environment.

**File server**

A device linked into a LAN, which is dedicated to storing public and private files for the network.

**File-sharing**

The ability to share files between multiple users.

**File specification**

Up to eight characters that identify a file.

**Filename**

A group of characters that identify a file saved to disk or tape.

**Footprint**

The space on a desk, table, or shelf occupied by a personal computer or work station and all related peripherals.

**Foreground task**

In a multitasking environment, the task with high priority is referred to as the foreground task. When competition arises between the foreground and background tasks over access to the CPU, the higher-priority task wins. Foreground tasks always win over background tasks.

**Gateway**

An access point from which a personal computer or network is linked to another network, mainframe, or data base.

| | |
|---|---|
| **Hard disk** | A device used to store data. It is composed of several platters with recording surfaces coated with magnetic oxide. The platters are similar to a diskette except they are rigid and store more data. A 10 megabyte hard disk can store data which would use 25 to 30 360K floppy diskettes. |
| **Hard-disk crash** | Typically, the failure of a hard-disk subsystem caused by the read-write head coming in destructive contact with one of the platters on which data is stored. |
| **Initialization** | The process by which diskettes are prepared to store data. On a double-sided double-density floppy disk, 40 electronic tracks are recorded to the disk and divided into sectors. IBM PC-DOS and MS-DOS use the Format command to initialize a disk. |
| **Initializing** | The process used by DOS to prepare diskettes to store data. See Initialization. |
| **Input** | The process of getting data into the computer. |
| **Interface** | The screen displays and commands that facilitate interaction between the user and the machine. |
| **Internal commands** | DOS commands that are resident in memory as soon as the system unit is booted. |
| **Kernel** | Portion of a program with operating-system-like code. |
| **Keyboard enhancer** | Software that redefines certain keys, at the user's discretion, to perform nonstandard operations. |
| **Local area network (LAN)** | A system in which multiple work stations are connected through cabling or telecommunications in order to provide file-sharing. |
| **Macro** | A collection of keystrokes. |
| **Manual backup systems** | Reverting to a manual, noncomputing mode of conducting business, i.e., paper-and-pencil operations. |
| **Media** | Types of cabling used on a local area network. |
| **Megabyte** | A measure of memory. One byte equals one character, one kilobyte equals 1024 bytes, and it takes 1024 kilobytes to equal one megabyte (in the simplest terms, 1,048,576 characters). |
| **MS-DOS** | Microsoft-disk operating system. |
| **Multiprocessing** | The capability of a computer to handle several users at one time. |
| **Multitasking** | The capability of a computer to handle several tasks at one time. |

| | |
|---|---|
| **Network administrator** | Person charged with maintaining the network system including issuing passwords, providing technical support, etc. |
| **Node** | One work station or personal computer on a local area network system. |
| **OS** | Operating system. See DOS. |
| **Output** | The process of getting data out of the computer. |
| **Parallel port** | An input or output port which handles eight bits of data simultaneously. |
| **Parameters** | Terms or items which modify a DOS command. |
| **Parity** | The use of an extra bit as an error checking strategy in each transmitted word. Depending upon system settings, parity is either even, odd, or no parity. Since each transmitted word is composed of bits set to either on (1) or off (0), the parity bit is set in such a way as to assure that every word is even (for even parity) or odd (for odd parity). If a word is received which does not match the system's parity, a message is sent to retransmit the word or block of data. |
| **PC** | A personal computer is a microcomputer or desk-top computer. |
| **PC-DOS** | IBM personal computer-disk operating system. |
| **Peripherals** | Devices attached to a computer which enable the input and output of data. Examples: printers, modems, plotters, disk drives. |
| **POST** | Power-on self-test, the self-diagnostic procedure a computer goes through when initially booted. |
| **Print queue** | A list of files to be printed. The queue is created by the Print command. |
| **Private volume** | A disk, directory, or subdirectory set aside for the exclusive use of a designated user on a local area network or multiuser system. Other users cannot access files on a private volume. |
| **Protocol** | The settings used for telecommunication of data. Protocol is set so the sending and receiving computers know what to expect in terms of word size, parity, and baud rate. |
| **Public volume** | A disk, directory, or subdirectory that may be accessed by any user on a local area network or multiuser system. Shared files and shared programs must reside on a public volume. |

| | |
|---|---|
| **RAM** | Random-access memory; the memory in a computer that can be manipulated or altered by loading a program, typing a document, or entering data. |
| **Read-and-write** | The ability to view and modify data. |
| **Read-only** | The ability only to view data. The user is restricted from modifying the data. |
| **Redundancy** | A concept used in disaster recovery planning that requires the duplication of hardware, software, and the periodic backup of data to insure that the business of an enterprise may continue with minimal disruption. |
| **Replaceable Parameters** | One of ten variables built into DOS for use with batch files. |
| **Restore** | The DOS command that uses files created by the Backup command and restores the data to a specified medium (diskette or hard-disk). |
| **ROM** | Read-only memory; the memory that never changes in a computer. Typically used to store instructions that the user cannot alter. |
| **Secondary storage** | Memory storage space located external to the CPU and its memory chips (tape backup, hard-disk, floppy disk). The term "storage" is synonymous with memory. |
| **Serial port** | Often referred to as an asynchronous port. Can transmit only one bit of data at a time. |
| **Standard devices** | Peripherals designated by DOS using reserved words. Standard devices include the console, parallel, and serial ports. |
| **Stopbits** | A bit sent to signal the end of a transmitted word, frame, or block of data. |
| **Switch** | Another term for a parameter. See Parameters. |
| **Terminal program** | A software program that facilitates the transfer of data through telecommunications. Typically these programs are menu-driven and provide an easy user interface for setting the telecommunications protocol, as well as storing commonly dialed phone numbers of on-line data bases and bulletin boards. |
| **Time-outs** | If a device does not respond to the CPU within a given period of time, a time-out error is generated. It means that a preset period of time has elapsed and control is returned to the CPU. |
| **Topology** | The pattern by which work stations are connected to a LAN. |

**Upward compatibility**      The assurance that new developments in hardware and software may be used by an older machine.

**User-friendly**            A term referring to the ease with which the user interfaces with the computer.

**Virtual drive**            A storage location such as a disk drive, which resides in an allocated part of memory. Data stored on a virtual drive is more volatile, but has faster access time than storage on a regular disk drive.

**Wildcard characters**      The asterisk and/or question mark, which may substitute for one or more characters in a filename used as part of a DOS command.

**Word size**                See Databits.

**Write-protect**            The ability only to view data. See Read-only.

APPENDIX

# B

# FDISK AND HARD DISK FORMATTING

Before you can use your hard disk it must be prepared to receive DOS. The Fdisk program will allow you to divide your hard disk into four partitions. A partition is an area of the hard disk which may have a different operating system. If you are going to have more than one operating system on your hard disk, you must have different partitions for them.

In this hard disk setup you are going to place DOS on a 10 megabyte hard disk and it will be the only operating system on the disk. Since you are going to only have DOS as the operating system on your disk, you will only need one partition.

## STARTING THE COMPUTER

1. Insert your DOS diskette into drive A:.

2. Turn on the computer.

3. Enter the current date and time.

## FDISK PROGRAM

4. Type FDISK .

5. Press <CR>.

The screen will display the response for the Fdisk command.  The Fdisk command will only give you a list of four choices to choose from when you only have one hard disk in your computer.

    IBM Personal Computer
    Fixed Disk Setup Program Version 3.10
        (C)Copyright IBM Corp. 1983,1985

    FDISK Options

    Choose one of the following:

            1.   Create DOS partition
            2.   Change Active Partition
            3.   Delete DOS Partition
            4.   Display Partition Data

    Enter choice: [1]

    Press ESC to return to DOS

 6. Press <CR> to pick the number (1) for your choice.

The screen will display the response for the number (1) choice to create a DOS partition.

    Create DOS Partition

    Do you wish to use the entire fixed
    disk for DOS (Y/N) ...............[Y]

    Press ESC to return to return to FDISK Operation

 7. Press <CR> to use the whole disk for the DOS operating system.

The screen will display the response for the request to use the entire fixed disk for DOS.

    Create DOS Partition

    Do you wish to use the entire fixed
    disk for DOS (Y/N) ...............[Y]

    System will now restart

    Insert DOS diskette in drive A:
    Press any key when ready

 8. Press any key to continue the Fdisk operation.

 9. Enter the current date and press <CR>.

 10. Enter the current time and press the <CR>..

The screen will display the following response.

    Current date is Tue  1-01-1980
    Enter new date (mm-dd-yy):11-15-85
    Current time is 0:51:23.40
    Enter new time: 18:00

    The IBM Personal Computer DOS
    Version 3.10 (C)Copyright International Business Machines Corp. 1981, 1985
                (C)Copyright Microsoft Corp. 1981, 1985

    A>_

**FORMAT FIXED DISK**

The hard disk is now prepared to receive DOS.  The Format command will place the DOS operating system onto the partition you created with the Fdisk command.

11. Your DOS diskette should be in drive A: .

12. Type **FORMAT C:/S/V**

13. Press <CR>.

14. Type **Y**

15. Press <CR>.

The screen displays the response for the start of the Format command.

    A>FORMAT C:/S/
    WARNING, ALL DATA ON NON-REMOVABLE DISK
    DRIVE C: WILL BE LOST!
    Proceed with Format (Y/N)?_

    Formatting..._

16. Type **Hard Disk** when the program asks for a Volume label.

17. Press <CR>.

The screen will display the following message upon completion of the Format command.

```
A>FORMAT C:/S/
WARNING, ALL DATA ON NON-REMOVABLE DISK
DRIVE C: WILL BE LOST!
Proceed with Format (Y/N)?_

Formatting...Format complete
System transferred

Volume label (11 characters, ENTER for none)? Hard Disk

10584064 bytes total disk space
   65536 bytes used by system
10518528 bytes available on disk


A>_
```

18. The Format command is now finished and you are ready to use your fixed disk.  Remove the DOS diskette from drive A: and reboot your computer.

# APPENDIX
# C

# SIMPLE DOS SHELL FILE LISTINGS

The following file listings will be helpful, if you choose to use a word processor rather than Edlin to create the files in the Guided Activity: Creating A Simple DOS Shell. These listings will also be helpful if you choose to use Edlin but not follow the step-by-step process outlined in unit 12. A few guidelines may help in the process.

1. The file contents must exactly match the listings below.

2. Give your files the same filenames listed here.

3. In the following listings, the first line indicates the filename under which the text file should be saved.

4. Save your files as ASCII text files, not as document files.

5. If blank lines must be included in a file, they are indicated as **<blank line>**.

6. If the TAB key should be hit to indent 8 spaces, it will be indicated by **<TAB>**. Multiple TABS will be indicated with multiple listings of **<TAB>**, for instance, **<TAB> <TAB> <TAB>** means the TAB key should be pressed three times.

After creating these files move them to the BATCH subdirectory created in steps 1-10 of the guided activity in unit 12. Complete the activity by returning to step 324 in the unit 12 exercise and follow the remaining steps.

```
Filename: 1.BAT


    ECHO OFF
    PROMPT $p$g
    CLS
    ECHO INSERT DISK TO BE FORMATTED IN DRIVE A:
    ECHO ANY DATA ON THE DISK WILL BE DESTROYED!
    PAUSE
    ECHO *
    ECHO * *
    ECHO * * *
    ECHO * * * * LAST CHANCE
    ECHO * * * * TO SAVE ANY DATA ON DISK IN DRIVE A:
    PAUSE
    ECHO * * * * *
    ECHO * * * * * *
    ECHO * * * * * * *
    ECHO * * * * * * * * TOO LATE!!.
    ECHO *
    ECHO * *
    ECHO * * *
    ECHO * * * *
    FORMAT A: <INPUTS
    MAINMENU
```

```
Filename: 2.BAT


    ECHO OFF
    PROMPT $p$g
    CLS
    TYPE BACKUP.SCR
    PROMPT ENTER LETTER OF CHOICE $g
```

```
Filename:  3.BAT


   ECHO OFF
   PROMPT $p$g
   CLS
```

```
Filename:  A.BAT


   ECHO OFF
   PROMPT $p$g
   CLS
   TYPE BACKUP.MSG
   PAUSE
   CLS
   BACKUP C:\ A:/S
   PAUSE
   MAINMENU
```

```
Filename:  B.BAT


   ECHO OFF
   PROMPT $p$g
   CLS
   TYPE BACKUP.MSG
   PAUSE
   CLS
   BACKUP C:\ A:/S/M
   PAUSE
   MAINMENU
```

```
Filename:  C.BAT


    ECHO OFF
    PROMPT $p$g
    CLS
    TYPE BACKUP.MSG
    PAUSE
    CLS
    TYPE BKUPSUB.SCR
    PROMPT TYPE "ONLY" AND SUBDIRECTORY NAME...PRESS RETURN $g
```

```
Filename:  D.BAT


    MAINMENU
```

```
Filename:  E.BAT


    ECHO OFF
    PROMPT $p$g
    CLS
```

```
Filename:  MAINMENU.SCR


   <blank line>
   <blank line>
   <blank line>
   <blank line>
   <TAB> <TAB> <TAB> A SIMPLE DOS SHELL
   <blank line>
   <TAB> <TAB> <TAB> 1.<TAB> Format A New Disk
   <blank line>
   <TAB> <TAB> <TAB> 2.<TAB> Backup Files
   <blank line>
   <TAB> <TAB> <TAB> 3.<TAB> Exit To DOS
   <blank line>
```

```
Filename:  MAINMENU.BAT


   ECHO OFF
   CLS
   TYPE MAINMENU.SCR
   PROMPT ENTER CHOICE BY NUMBER $g
```

---

Filename:  BACKUP.SCR


&lt;blank line&gt;
&lt;blank line&gt;
&lt;blank line&gt;
&lt;blank line&gt;
&lt;TAB&gt; &lt;TAB&gt; &lt;TAB&gt;  BACKUP SUB-MENU
&lt;blank line&gt;
&lt;TAB&gt; &lt;TAB&gt; &lt;TAB&gt;  A. &lt;TAB&gt;  Backup ALL Files On Hard Disk
&lt;blank line&gt;
&lt;TAB&gt; &lt;TAB&gt; &lt;TAB&gt;  B. &lt;TAB&gt;  Backup ONLY Modified Hard Disk Files
&lt;blank line&gt;
&lt;TAB&gt; &lt;TAB&gt; &lt;TAB&gt;  C. &lt;TAB&gt;  Backup Files In A Subdirectory
&lt;blank line&gt;
&lt;TAB&gt; &lt;TAB&gt; &lt;TAB&gt;  D. &lt;TAB&gt;  Return To Main Menu
&lt;blank line&gt;
&lt;TAB&gt; &lt;TAB&gt; &lt;TAB&gt;  E. &lt;TAB&gt;  Exit To DOS
&lt;blank line&gt;
&lt;blank line&gt;

---

Filename:  BACKUP.MSG


&lt;blank line&gt;
&lt;blank line&gt;
&lt;blank line&gt;
&lt;blank line&gt;
&lt;TAB&gt; &lt;TAB&gt; &lt;TAB&gt;  All files will be backed up to drive A:
&lt;blank line&gt;
&lt;TAB&gt; &lt;TAB&gt; &lt;TAB&gt;  Be sure you have a sufficient number of
&lt;TAB&gt; &lt;TAB&gt; &lt;TAB&gt;  blank formatted diskettes.  It can take
&lt;TAB&gt; &lt;TAB&gt; &lt;TAB&gt;  25 diskettes to back up 10 megabytes of data.
&lt;blank line&gt;
&lt;blank line&gt;

```
Filename:  BKUPSUB.SCR


    <blank line>
    <blank line>
    <blank line>
    <blank line>
    <TAB> <TAB> <TAB> This menu option will allow you to make a
    <TAB> <TAB> <TAB> complete backup of any ONE subdirectory.
    <blank line>
    <TAB> <TAB> <TAB> In order to begin the backup operation,
    <TAB> <TAB> <TAB> simply type the subdirectory name preceded
    <TAB> <TAB> <TAB> by the word ONLY (for example: ONLY DOS).
    <blank line>
    <TAB> <TAB> <TAB> This option will only work for subdirectories
    <TAB> <TAB> <TAB> immediately under the Root directory.
```

```
Filename:  ONLY.BAT


    ECHO OFF
    BACKUP C:\%1 A:/S
    PROMPT $p$g
    PAUSE
    MAINMENU
```

# INDEX

640K
  maximum addressable memory p 13

<Back Space>
  erase incorrect characters p 140

**A**

Advanced DOS 1.x
  p 260
  address 16 meg of RAM p 260
  multitasking p 260
  new operating system p 256

Alternative Processing strategies
  p 188

ASCII collating sequence
  p 142

ASCII value
  p 142

Assign
  p 196

Asynchronous port
  protocol p 166

Attrib
  archival bit p 227
  boilerplate documents p 205
  copied files p 205
  global wildcards p 205
  p 204
  read-and-write bit p 204
  read-only files p 206
  write-protected p 205

Attribute bit
  p 191

Autoexec Bat
  p 108

Hard-disk failure
 causes p 189

**I**

IBM DOS
 PC-DOS p 7

IBM PC
 revision B p 13

Internal commands
 list p 14
 resident in RAM p 13

**J**

Join
 p 196

**K**

Keyboard enhancer
 p 227

**L**

LAN
 Fcbs p 218
 data sharing p 216
 disk server p 216
 file server p 216
 gateway p 217
 local area network p 216
 nodes p 217
 shared peripherals p 216
 wide area network p 216

Laser printer
 p 217

Lastdrive
 default value p 220
 Lastdrive p 217
 maximum on system p 219
 p 219
 syntax p 221

Local area network
 LAN p 216
 no uniform standard p 216
 p 216
 private directories p 220
 public directories p 220

**M**

Macro creation
 p 228

Md
 p 12

Megabyte
 p 257

Memory
 addressed by Intel 80286 p 257
 addressed by Intel 8088 p 257
 expanded p 257
 extended memory p 257
 extended p 257

Memory-Resident Programs
 p 257
 p 196

Menu generators
 p 226

Method of interface
 serial or parallel p 132

Mkdir
 p 12
 p 115

Notes

Notes

Notes

Notes

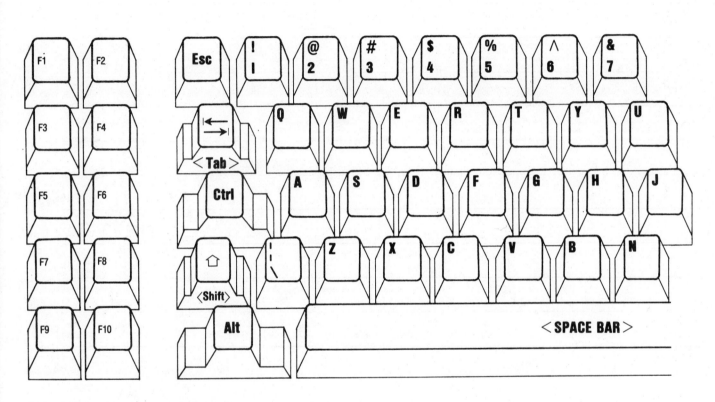

## MS–DOS®/PC–DOS KEYBOARD

F1   Playback last command, character by character

F2   Playback last command up to a specific character

F3   Playback repeats entire last command

F4   Skip characters in last command up to a specified character

F5   Saves currently displayed line for editing and advances to next line

F6   Generates an end-of-file mark (Ctrl Z)

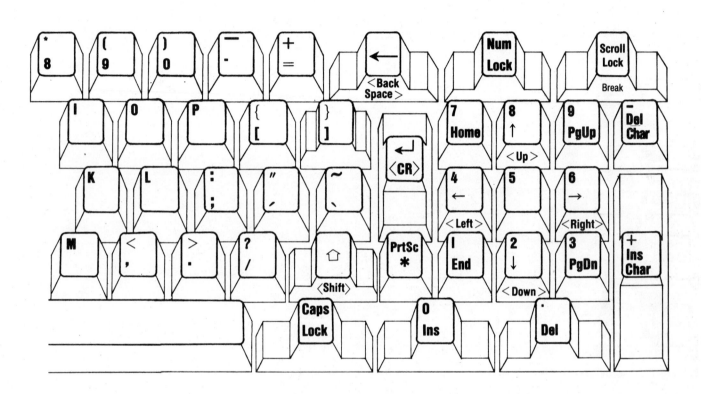

## IBM PC™ Abbreviations

Esc—Escape Key

Ctrl or Λ —Control Key

Alt—Alternate Key

Num Lock—Number Lock Key

Pg Up—Page Up Key

PrtSc—Print Screen Key

Pg Dn—Page Down Key

Ins— Insert Character

Del— Delete Character